OWN IT

TRIGGER™
The mental health & wellbeing publisher

OWN IT

Endorsements

"*Jess is funny, relatable and has changed my outlook on self-love. She helped me see that true self-compassion is about treating ourselves with the respect, understanding and kindness we deserve.*"
Giovanna Fletcher, *Sunday Times* bestselling author and host of the *Happy Mum Happy Baby* podcast, @mrsgifletcher

"*Jess is a powerhouse who has gone on such a transformation in her own life. It's wonderful that she is now able to teach people how to do the same with this book. In every area of life, Jess Owns It – she's a woman who practices what she preaches! The world needs more women like Jess.*"
Michelle Elman, author of *The Joy of Being Selfish*, @scarrednotscared

"*Reading this was like getting a pep talk from a friend. I loved it!*"
Fiona Thomas, author of *Out of Office*, @fionalikestoblog

About the Author

Award-winning blogger, confidence and self-love advocate, and motivational comedian Jessica Jones runs the popular Instagram account @TheFatFunnyOne and podcast *Say It With Your Whole Chest*, where she shares her inspiring journey from self-loathing to acceptance and inner confidence.

Not afraid to bear all, Jess shows women they can love themselves at any size with stretch marks, scars, cellulite and all. She's a firm believer that true self-love is attainable for anyone, and a happy over-sharer of her perfectly imperfect life in Bedfordshire, UK, with her husband, three (nearly four) kids and pup.

OWN IT

How to Build Confidence, Love Yourself & Embrace Your Body

By Jessica Jones

AKA The Fat Funny One

TRIGGER™

The mental health & wellbeing publisher

This edition published in 2023 by Trigger Publishing
An imprint of Shaw Callaghan Ltd

UK Office
The Stanley Building
7 Pancras Square
Kings Cross
London N1C 4AG

US Office
On Point Executive Center, Inc
3030 N Rocky Point Drive W
Suite 150
Tampa, FL 33607
www.triggerhub.org

Text Copyright © 2022 Jessica Jones
First published in 2022 by Welbeck Balance

A CIP catalogue record for this book is available upon request from the British Library
ISBN: 978-1-83796-290-7
Ebook ISBN: 978-1-83796-291-4

Cover design by Studio Nic & Lou
Cover photograph by Kelly Reeves Photography
Typeset by Lapiz Digital Services

To the me who needed this book all those years ago. I wish you would see your potential, see past the heartbreak and the pain, see past the bits of you that you're currently tearing apart, and understand just how incredible life is going to be when you just start to Own It.

Contents

Introduction

If you're anything like me, you may have spent the majority of your time here on Earth wondering why you just can't get life quite "right". Whether it's relationships (romantic or otherwise), sticking to a diet, feeling good in what you wear, landing the dream job or becoming debt-free (or at least having a handle on the desperate need to shop to fill a void), it might have always felt like you're failing – at something? As if you're never quite "good enough"?

And often when one thing starts to go a *little bit* well, it can feel like it soon all comes crashing back down, leaving you wondering why you even bothered in the first place. Sound familiar?

For me, life has often felt like a ridiculous uphill battle. A mountain that I just couldn't manage to climb in order to live the life I really wanted.

I would see other people living what seemed like these "dream lives" and wonder how they got it all together so well. Meanwhile, I'd be stuck in a hamster wheel of self-doubt, low self-esteem and, quite frankly, at times, pure dread over what was going to happen next.

If, like me, you have spent years feeling that happiness, joy and success are reserved for everyone but you, this is the book for you.

Here, I share just how broken I felt for most of my life and how – by taking hold of the mess that I felt my life was, and truly OWNING IT (see page 8) – I went on a journey of total transformation from feeling defeated, overwhelmed and helpless in my five-foot-two (1.57m), size 18 (UK) body, to feeling confident, happy and like anything is possible (stretch marks, cellulite, wobbly bits 'n' all)!

My hope is that the mix of honest insights and practical ideas within the book will empower you to take actions that will help *you* to turn *your* life around, too, so you can feel the glow of inner confidence that you deserve to feel in everyday life – simply by making the decision to OWN IT.

It sounds so dramatic (I know!). Believe me, I had read all the books, followed all the blogs and listened to all the podcasts where people would make statements like that. And each time I would roll my eyes and say, "Yeah, I'm glad it worked for them. But it won't work for me!"

Yet here I am, with everything crossed that this book will show you that it really *can* work for *you*, *too* – and that if change is within *my* reach, then it's within *your* reach too, if you want it.

For such a long time, I was aware of voices in my head constantly telling me that I "wasn't enough" – echoes of the voice of the teacher who told me I'd never "succeed", of the ex-partner who made horrible comments about my body, and of the various other critics and bullies I met along life's path … But I realized after a lot of soul-searching that by far the loudest and most negative voice was *my own* and that *that* was the voice I needed to change. And, luckily for me – and now you, too – *that* is the voice that we have the *power to change.*

THE ART OF TRANSFORMATION

When I was a teenager, one of my favourite things to do was to give my room a makeover. I'd always start by moving my very wonky and questionably stable Ikea furniture around for the hundredth time. I would then change up the posters on my walls and maybe – if I was lucky – paint a feature wall with tester pots or a random old paint tin I found in the garage.

When it was all done, and everything was exactly where I wanted to be, it felt like a totally new space. The same room that I had felt bored, frustrated or annoyed in was transformed – and everything felt brand new. I would leave my bedroom, closing the door behind me, and stand in the hallway for a minute before walking back in to really take in the change and relish in the transformation. Every time I walked in, a wave of joy would come over me.

However, despite the sense of elation each time I completed one of these "makeover missions", the process of *getting* to this point was always pretty overwhelming and frustrating. I would unpack *everything*. Empty every drawer, go through all my clothes, re-read every notebook and old journal, try on every old lip gloss found ... And hours after I had started, I would stand in the middle of a mound of complete chaos, wondering why the heck I had started this process in the first place – full of regret for ever having thought that change was a good idea.

My journey to self-confidence and self-love has really been no different to that of my room transformations. After years of self-doubt and self-hatred, I got to a point where I was *desperate* for change. But when I started to unpack my emotions and the parts of my life that I had buried deep, I found myself in the middle of a complete mess of emotions (regrets, fears, insecurities and all the rest ...), wondering why the heck I had ever started this process in the first place!

I was overwhelmed. What I had felt compelled to do suddenly felt insurmountable and impossible. But, just like in my experiences with my room, I had to trust that the end result would be worth it. Plus, to be honest, I felt that I didn't have much choice but to persevere now that I was at this stage of the chaos!

But it turns out that I didn't realize just how much of a transformation *would* take place in the end ...

Now, a decade or so on, just like when I used to walk into my newly transformed room in awe of the change, I wake up every day in a life that feels so good, I can't quite believe it is mine. And when I remember that it *is* – and that I have created this – a wave of joy comes rolling in around me. A feeling that makes me know it was all worth it.

I am a Mum of three – soon to be four – Sophia, Isabella, Jaycen and Baby Boy. They are the lights of my life but also the reason I drink way too much coffee and have a wine subscription. My husband, Trevor, and I have been together for just over ten years. We won't talk about the "Ross and Rachel" break we had, so let's just call it a round decade. And because our house isn't chaotic enough, we also have three beautiful fur babies – our two cats Stuffy and Pumpkin, and our wild but incredible Labrador, Marshall. Our house is chaos but we wouldn't have it any other way, as, thankfully, I no longer feel the same constant chaos on the *inside* that I used to feel.

Oh, and I still love a good makeover programme, by the way – or (given we're no longer in the '90s) a good interior design social media page! – as they remind me of the endless potential for incredible change in our lives.

ACCEPTING THAT WE'RE ENOUGH

A few years ago I came across one of my boxes of old journals one day and began flicking through the ratty pages that were covered with barely readable handwriting and water smudges from tears …

16 June 2011
I am disgusting. I actually cannot even look at myself in the mirror. I covered the one up in the hallway, as I just don't even want to see what is looking back at me. It actually makes me want to be sick. I make myself sick. Why won't anyone just love me? Am I really that bad? Of course I am. I see everyone else in their perfect relationships and just wish it was me. I wish I could be loved too. I wish someone wouldn't just use me, then dump me. I wish I looked like all the women who have men at their feet and don't have

to beg for just a small bit of attention like I do. Gosh, I am so pathetic! Oh, and I quit my job! I say "quit"! In reality, I was about to be fired, so I quickly handed in my notice to save myself even more embarrassment. They all hate me. I could tell they were always talking about me and didn't like me. So, where does that leave me now? I have no job. I am broke, ugly and fat. Nobody is going to want me. I am never going to be like the other women – I have tried. I have tried but I just keep stuffing myself! Argh! WHY AM I LIKE THIS? Literally, what is the point? What am I going to do? I have nothing. I am so angry at myself. I am so disappointed. I am a disappointment. I just don't want to do this anymore. I don't want to be here anymore. I am not worth it.

This is just a snippet of one of dozens of similar diary entries. Sharp, negative, painful and ugly. For years, I scrawled pages and pages of journals with this kind of frustration, anger and self-hatred.

I was deep in my own victimhood – convinced that the reason nothing was working for me was because I simply wasn't *enough*. I wasn't clever enough, slim enough, funny enough, brave enough or rich enough. I wasn't enough for anyone or anything. I didn't know at the time that I wasn't alone in feeling these things. And that I was experiencing what many people do: low self-worth, lack of self-esteem and the anxiety that can come with these.

Finding and reading my journal that day a few years back threw me right back to my darkest days of self-loathing. But as I read on, I saw the beginning of a huge change that was coming. Through the harsh words of self-criticism, I saw the slow realization that in order for me to get myself together and feeling better, I was going to have to start picking things up, one at a time, and dealing with them, rather than trying to ignore them or push them away. Only then would I be able to create a happier space, and happier life, for myself. I needed to understand how to manage my anxiety, take time to build my self-esteem and confidence, and I needed to know – and *believe* – that I was worth it.

So, in 2014, that's exactly what I did. I started making a dent in the life-mess that I had allowed to build up, gently letting go of the circumstances and people that no longer served me. I started making room for more positivity to come into my life. I began prioritizing the things that were most important to me. And, most importantly, I started to work on totally and completely accepting myself as I was at that very moment.

I had a deep craving and a sense of desperation to finally be able to live life to the full and stop tearing myself apart at every moment.

I couldn't shake the inner voice that told me, despite all the negatives, that I deserved *more*. That I *was* enough – even amid all the chaos of life.

I knew if I wanted to really enjoy and feel excited about every day, I needed to make changes *now*, before I lost any more time living a *shadow* of a life. If I wanted a chance to truly live and love life, then I needed to stand in the disarray and OWN IT!

So, How Do You OWN IT?

To OWN IT is to live unapologetically.

To be entirely comfortable with who you are.

To love yourself enough that you don't seek approval from anywhere other than from inside yourself.

To Own It is to be accountable for your own life, for your own behaviour.

To know that you have a choice to either live overwhelmed by shame from the things you have done in the past, or to accept that your past is part of who you are but doesn't define you; in fact, it shapes you to be the badass person you are right now, in this very moment.

Owning It isn't about trying to reach a state of perfection or any particular goal that has been painted to us as the "perfect" way to live, the "perfect" body to have, the perfect clothes to wear ...

Neither is it about "fixing" everything. Rather it is about recognizing that, while there is healing to be done, *you are not broken.*

Owning It is about *acceptance* – being happy with yourself, in any circumstance, because you know that there is more for you out there and you truly believe you deserve it.

THE IMPORTANCE OF EVERYDAY DECISIONS

Life whizzes by, and in the age of instant messaging and same-day online grocery deliveries, we have become used to things happening *quickly*. As a result, we are often impatient. We want change overnight. We want instant results from big, quick, simple decisions. But when it comes to changing the way you think about yourself, that's just not the way it works.

It is said that the average adult makes around 35,000 decisions a day – thirty-five *thousand*! And there was me thinking that just one or two big simple ones would automatically transform my life!

Instead, I realized, on my journey from self-loathing to self-acceptance, that it was, in fact, many *small* decisions made every hour, every day, every week, every month that would lead me to Own It. Hundreds of small, consistent choices that would add up to make a *huge* difference over time. Small shifts in mindset and behaviour that have the power to change your internal dialogue with pretty immediate results. Changes in what social media you consume – or how much of it. How much time you spend on your phone. The type of language you use when you talk to yourself ...

It's committing to small but significant choices like these that transformed my life into one that I now feel so happy and contented in. And that I hope will bring you that same kind of happiness, fulfilment and sense of thriving.

PLANNING YOUR JOURNEY

I recently had to explain to my eldest daughter, Sophia, that we didn't always have sat navs or other tech that allowed us to just type in a location and see how far away it was, with options of the routes to get there. It wasn't quite that easy.

Instead, in London, we had something called an *A to Z*. She was confused and, to be honest, so was I as I tried to explain it to her. I explained that it was a small pocket-size book of maps (if you were lucky) or a *huge* A2 book, like the one my grandad got me to celebrate me finally passing my driving test!

If you were going somewhere you didn't know, you had to look up the road name at the back of the book and then find the page number. Once you located that, you were given a grid reference in the form of a number and a letter that represented the section of the page it was on. You then had to locate the road name (which was often abbreviated) within that square. And only *then* would you be able to work out how to get there from wherever you were.

She was horrified and said, "I wouldn't go anywhere if it was that hard Mummy!" I laughed and explained that we didn't know any different and so, to us, this was just how we got to the places we wanted to go.

Making a decision to transform your life – and unlearning all the negative things you believe to be true about yourself – is not unlike this! We never want to set out for our destination if it feels too hard to get to, if we feel like it's too complicated or if we have an overwhelming fear we are going to get lost. But, like when we had no other option than to search grid numbers in a tatty old book, it gets to the point where we realize that we have no other option but to break down the walls we have closed in on ourselves and start planning our routes and taking the first steps. After all, what's the alternative? Just staying stuck in the same place for the rest of our lives? That wouldn't be great, would it?

When I first started on my journey, a part of me seemed to think that it would be as simple as telling myself I was a badass in the mirror three times a day. I almost want to laugh now at how ridiculous that seems – as if I could just change my mind about the things that made me who I was as easily as changing my nail polish colour. If it was this easy, then why wasn't everyone living their best, limitless life, smashing their goals and walking around like they own the place? Well, that's because it isn't that easy. The journey can be complicated and split across multiple pages of your A2-sized A to Z!

It's important to know from the start that you will take wrong turns, hit dead ends and go round roundabouts of self-sabotage more times than you can count. But unless you get in the car and actually start the journey, you won't get any further than the place you are in now.

The journey to truly believing in yourself, loving yourself unconditionally and getting the most from your life comes with a lot of work. But it's so worth it as you gradually get closer to where you want to be and how you want to feel.

In this book I will share with you how I managed to clear, organize and transform my "room" – aka my life – into one that I truly love being in. I will share my personal mental health journey and the impact that my negative – and positive – thoughts have had.

I will show you how you can take the first steps on your own journey toward a more positive mindset. I will share with you the skills and practices that I have learned over the years and show you that it's possible for *you*, too, to find inner confidence and truly accept yourself.

Gradually, you will come to understand how you can unapologetically embrace yourself and your incredible body and mind – and love yourself wholeheartedly.

I share all this openly, honestly and candidly with you as I want you to know that *you are not alone* and change really *is* possible.

Learning to authentically Own yourself, as you are, is a life-changing decision. It will mean:

- Uncomfortable conversations with both yourself and others (talking to yourself is totally cool by the way!)
- Letting go of things that have happened in the past and stepping out of shame
- Facing fears and feelings that you have buried deep
- Giving yourself time to heal
- Making small decisions *every single day* that lead you to taking small actions in line with the life you want to lead – and are excited to wake up to each morning
- Giving yourself permission to take the power back in your life
- Creating a life moving forward that is about *your best you*

I know that, depending on where you are in your journey, this might feel impossible right now – as far-fetched as comfy high heels. But try to show yourself the love and compassion that you would show your best mate. Take a moment to encourage yourself, as you would your friend, to at least make the first small decision to try – and to really *believe* that this change is possible.

IT STARTS WITH SELF-COMPASSION

Every one of us is trying our best. So, before we get into the nitty gritty of how to start Owning It, the first thing I want you to do is to let go of any guilt you hold for being in the place that you are right now. Your current situation does not determine where you can go and the possibilities that could happen from here; it only determines the place in which you start.

The very fact that this book has made it into your hands means you have already decided you want something better for yourself, which means that you are further ahead in your journey to loving yourself than you might think!

The fact that you woke up this morning is all the evidence you need that you are worthy of life and that there is opportunity for change. We are often so quick to show compassion to others – friends, family and often even strangers – yet we are slow to show *ourselves* the same compassion (if ever).

So show it to yourself now. Give yourself the opportunity to let go of the difficult feelings, to stop being so hard on yourself and to focus on where you can go from here.

STEPPING INTO YOUR POWER

"Powerful" was never a word I would have used to describe myself at all. In my mind, that word was reserved for the billionaires and superheroes, right? Wrong!

True power isn't about how much money or status you have. And it certainly isn't about being able to control other people's actions (that's impossible). On my journey, I have found that true power lies in loving yourself unconditionally – so that you are able to live a full and happy life, and others can see the light shine from inside of you.

It's about owning your innate power so that you can be the person you want to be, are capable of being and absolutely deserve to be.

ABOUT THIS BOOK

I have divided this book into six main chapters, each covering a different area of life that had a huge impact on how I felt about myself. On speaking to others, I found that these were common themes that most people related to, so I hope that you will relate to at least one, if not all, of them:

1. Breaking Free from Limiting Beliefs
2. Finding & Stepping into Your Confidence
3. Learning to Accept, Like & Love Yourself
4. Dealing with "Mean Girls" & Naysayers
5. Embracing Your Body & Loving the Skin You're In
6. Successfully Navigating the Sea of Social Media

And I then round things up at the end with a section of final reflections and tips, inspired by my dear friend Emma, called "The Golden Nugget of Owning It".

By sharing my experiences, my hope is that you will come to understand that I have been in situations that have completely destroyed my sense of self-belief and created a mindset so negative that I didn't ever think happiness was going to be something I could obtain. Yet I *did* obtain it – and *you* can too.

I read somewhere once that there is someone in the world who would drown in their own tears if not for seeing yours. This book is me sharing my tears with you in the hope that I am able to help you silence that voice in your mind that tells you that you aren't good enough.

I want to amplify the voice that tells you that *you are amazing just as you are*.

But that voice isn't going to be mine – it's going to be *yours*. This voice may be very quiet at the moment. You might not be able to hear it at all. But I am hoping that, as you work your way through the book, it will get louder and clearer. And, after a while, it will be the voice that you hear the most often and the loudest.

I want you to get up, grab life and start really Owning every step you make from here.

IT'S TIME TO TAKE ACTION

Reflecting on the dark times of my journey while writing this book hasn't been easy, But the real work from here on in isn't for me to do; it is for *you* to do (sorry!). I have already done mine!

You can read all the books and post all the inspirational quotes in the world, but if you don't put into action the things you learn as you read, then you won't get anywhere. That's some tough love right there! But I want to be real with you.

I spent soooo much time reading self-help books, and then wondering why I wasn't seeing any change. It was because I wasn't making the decision to put any of the information and guidance I had read into *practice*.

At the end of each main chapter I have therefore included:

- An "Owning It Top Tip" – to give you a point of focus
- "Self-Reflection Questions" – to empower you to really think, and start answering questions for yourself, about your *own* journey through life

and

- "GUIDED TASKS" – practical exercises to support you on your journey; these are all activities that I have done myself, as part of *my* healing journey, and that have been so beneficial to me in learning how to Own It that I felt I needed to share them with you, too.

Take your time with all of these. Come back to them if you need to. Feel free to do them over and over again. There is no right or wrong. This is about you and is personal to you – so don't overthink it, don't worry about it. Just work through things at your own pace and in your own style. *Doing* this work is key because change can't come if you just *will* it to.

It doesn't matter how long you have felt stuck in a negative place. We aren't here to dwell on that. We are here to focus on making a *shift* – so that you can be fully present in the *now*. So that you can enjoy every moment from here on in because *you deserve it.*

FINDING YOUR CATALYST

My personal journey of growth happens to run directly parallel to becoming a mother. I met my now-husband, Trevor, almost exactly a month to the day after the diary entry that I shared with you earlier was written. This encounter was one of the first events that triggered a huge change for me. I met Trevor on a night out in July 2011; best not do the maths but Sophia (our eldest child) was born in August 2012.

Don't get me wrong, I am categorically *not* telling everyone to go out on a wild night out, meet a guy and get pregnant within the first few months in order to ignite a life-changing moment! Absolutely not! I'd suggest *enjoying* living that single life – savouring uninterrupted sleep and lie-ins, going to the supermarket solo, and having the freedom to do a poo alone! But meeting Trevor, getting pregnant and becoming a mother just happened to be the catalysts for the change in *my* life. So many others I know have had different catalysts in *their* lives, such as grief, a change in career, the loss of a job, illness, or even a break-up. There are countless moments in life that can be catalysts for change. Yours doesn't have to be the same as anyone else's. What matters is that we all get to the point where we just know that *change is needed.*

I had only known Trevor for five months when I found out that I was pregnant. It didn't feel like an ideal situation at the time. I was 22, living in a flat above a shop that had horrendous damp and no heating. I was in mountains of debt, behind on the rent and working a temp job that was due to end within the next two months – so I had no job security either. Like I said, not an ideal situation! Trevor was midway through university and hadn't even met my Mum yet. So it was a shock to say the least! But I also had this sense deep down that "This is going to change everything" and "It's all going to be alright". But let me be clear – this was *way deep down* because on the surface I was freaking *out*!

I was going to have this new small person to provide for – not just financially but emotionally too! How on earth was I going to do that when I was defaulting on the rent (again) and was still trying to figure out who the heck I was!?

GETTING TO KNOW YOUR EGO

I am pretty good at getting practical, at finding solutions to deal with the surface-level stuff, so I did all that I could do make sure we had what was required and to give our pending arrival everything that she needed. (They don't need a baby wipe warmer FYI.) I worked several jobs, sold almost everything I owned for cash and generally just did whatever it took. After five years I had managed to claw my way out of debt and get myself in a better financial position – "for the sake of my family". But it was in 2014, when I found myself in therapy following being bullied at work that the dots got fully connected and I realized just how much of my life was still based around fulfilling my own personal ego.

Ego: something I didn't think I had because all I associated that word with was men who had big ones – and who tended to be estate agents or models! (No offence to anyone in those job roles. I totally know different now). The point is that I didn't think ego was something I had! But I did have one, of course. And I still do. We all do! It isn't just reserved for big, cocky business people!

Our ego is how we see ourselves. It is the part of our mind that identifies with certain beliefs, traits and habits. And while I had always had this idea of it being the thing that made people arrogant or selfish, I soon began to realize that it also has many other effects on how we present ourselves and how we feel.

I began to see that my ego was at play all over the place. When I was, for example, craving gossip and then feeling elevated by being part of it. When I felt jealous that others were more "successful" than me. When I blamed everyone and everything *else* for things that were going wrong in my life. When I allowed negative circumstances to fuel the drama that made me feel like "someone". And so much more ...

EMBRACING AUTHENTICITY

Before getting to this revelation about myself (and my ego), I had felt for such a long time that there was a big part of me that so wanted to really *Own* who I was, the life I was living and the circumstances that surrounded me.

I wanted to be able to feel confident, happy and *free*, and to share completely openly and honestly with others. But I didn't feel I could do that by just being "Jess", as I was so stuck telling myself that I wasn't good enough, that no one would accept me and that I needed to change to be worthy of being liked.

So, in 2014, I made the decision to create another version of me to fit with the more open, fully authentic person I wanted to be – and to start sharing my journey, and my vulnerability, on social media. And that's how "The Fat Funny One" was born – a name by which I've been known online ever since.

What started as an account of my attempts to lose weight (I was struggling big time with body image among everything else at the time) – slowly but surely shifted over time into a space for me to really push myself to be the most authentic version of myself publicly on *lots* of different levels. And to Own It more broadly.

Now, over 100,000 followers and counting later, there is an incredible online community surrounding The Fat Funny One, which has made me realize just how important sharing our journeys with one another really is. And just what a big impact the simple decision to share our authenticity can have.

WHERE I AM NOW

Never in my wildest dreams did I think I would ever describe myself as "confident". But I can now honestly (and *confidently!*) say that I am indeed confident, happy and finally Owning exactly who I am – and it is the most liberating place to be.

I count my lucky stars for this. I thank myself every day for being brave enough to set out on the road to self-discovery and recovery. I don't think I would be here with my family all thriving, shouting and causing havoc if I hadn't.

I am proud to say that I finally feel at home – with work, family, life and career. I feel like I am exactly where I am supposed to be and doing exactly what I am meant to be doing.

The drive and passion that I have for empowering others (in the way that I discovered that I could empower myself) has now spilled into so many other areas of my life. I continue to share my journey with others online. I have written this book (which I hope serves you well). And, after working in recruitment for the best part of 12 years (it's always been about people for me!), I have now also trained as a Performance and Life Coach so that I can continue to do what it takes to encourage others to see the potential – and the light – that they have in themselves.

I often have days where I wonder if this is really my life. I have gone from the girl who was in debt, settling for relationships that broke me, being bullied and wondering what was ever going to come of my life (with self-esteem at an all-time low) – to waking up each day to a family and career that I adore, but *most importantly* waking up and loving *myself*.

It didn't happen overnight, and it took patience and commitment. But how I did it is ultimately pretty simple, which is why I want to share it with you in this book.

I've had to work on giving myself permission to enjoy my life as it is *now* and accept that it is real – reminding myself that I *deserve* the joy that I feel and the sense of pride about how far I have come.

So here I am – Owning my messy, chaotic and imperfect but *happy* life.

Owning my soft, saggy, wobbly and fluffy body.

Owning my past, including my mistakes, and my now.

And sitting so comfortably in that, that I feel like I am finally living!

I want this for you too.

And I believe that you can get there, because if *I* can, *you* can.

So are you ready to Own It?

Chapter 1

Breaking Free from Limiting Beliefs

Where are you in your journey to Owning It? Maybe you've made a concerted effort to start learning how to love parts of yourself, have read countless self-help books, and are looking for a boost or some further understanding of how to take things to the next stage? Or maybe you are at the very start of your journey, laden with negative thoughts, and just don't feel that self-love or confidence are things you will ever be able to obtain, no matter how hard you try?

Regardless of where you are, I'm going to take a guess at something that you're probably feeling given you've picked up this book – and that's fed up!

I remember *so* vividly the feeling of being utterly fed up with feeling so low. I so badly wanted to change. I yearned to feel happiness like I saw in others. But I couldn't see the point in doing anything about it as I felt that it was never going to be possible for *me* to change things and feel good.

On the surface (to friends, family and others I met), I may have always *seemed* happy and smiling. But, deep down, I wasn't *feeling* happy.

I have often joked that my life was so full of drama that it could totally be a Netflix series (any producers out there feel free to hit me up!). But by 2014, the pressure of it all got too much, with the tipping point being a breakdown in my relationship with Trevor, resulting in the Ross and Rachel-style break that I mentioned earlier. The constant feeling that I was living in a soap opera was so overwhelming that I felt like I was going crazy.

I got to a point where it became apparent to both myself and those around me that I was unable to deal with the dark cloud over my head on my own anymore. I was signed off work due to stress (I had been working as an administrator following my return to work after having Sophia in 2012). And I was given an opportunity to speak to a therapist through work services. At first, I declined, because, in *my* head, therapy was for people who had "real problems", and I couldn't see that in myself despite knowing full well that something didn't feel right.

But as the overwhelm took more and more hold over my life – and I could barely recognize myself any longer – I made the decision to attend the six-week therapy course that had been offered to me. And I have been going ever since – that's seven years now, and counting!

Before this, when people had spoken to me about therapy, I imagined it would be how I had seen it in the movies: in a big luxurious room with a grand mahogany desk, floor-to-ceiling windows and certificates in frames on the walls noting the countless qualifications my therapist had. My therapist would sit up straight in a tall-backed armchair (comfortable but not *too comfy*), with one smartly dressed leg draped over the other, and a notepad balanced on their lap. Opposite would sit a chocolate-brown chaise longue where I would lie down dramatically and answer the only question I thought they would ask me: "And how does that make you feel?".

In reality, while my therapist *did* sit as I imagined, with a notepad on her lap, the sessions were in what looked like an ordinary doctor's office (nothing grand about it!). And we talked about all sorts of background life stuff – such as where I was from and seemingly random things from my childhood.

At first, I couldn't understand how any of it was relevant to the things I was thinking, feeling and experiencing *now*, so I became frustrated that I wasn't getting answers to all my problems straightaway! But when I told my therapist this, she said something that not only made complete sense at the time but that has transformed my life since.

She said: "Jess, in order to help you move forward, I need to know where you have come *from*. Your childhood is where you learned how to feel. It's the start of your story."

I didn't get it at first, because it seemed so counterproductive to look back when all the positive quotes I had read and all the motivational speakers I had watched said things like, "Don't look back as it's not the direction you're going. Focus on your future. You are not your past …"

But I soon came to understand the reality that *every* past experience I had ever lived through had played a part in who I had become and who I was becoming. As such, the beliefs that I now held – many of which had been created in childhood – were fundamental in how I was behaving, and feeling, as an adult.

So, unless I brought these beliefs (particularly any that were holding me back) to the surface, unpacked them and got them in check, I was never going to be able to see any *real* change in the mess that I felt my life was.

This is all part of the process that *you* will go through, too, which is why this chapter is dedicated to recognizing your own key limiting beliefs, identifying how they're playing out in your life and starting to face them head on by reframing them.

I'm going to share in the pages that follow my thoughts, feelings and learnings as I went through this process myself, as it has been fundamental in me coming to understand who I am, *why* I am who I am, where I belong, and what I can *be* and *do* moving forward (answer: anything I like!).

THE POWER OF OUR BELIEFS

Did you know that our underlying beliefs are the main driver behind any decision we make throughout our lives? As such, understanding what, why and how you believe the things you do is key to making lasting change as it will help you to understand the reasons behind the decisions you make – and whether or not they are right for you.

Beliefs are attitudes or convictions that something is true. They give us the principles we live by – an idea of how we "should" live based on what we know about the world at the point when the beliefs are formed.

However, we are children when many of our beliefs are forged; Bruce Lipton, author of bestselling book *The Biology of Belief* (Hay House, 2015) discusses how, up to around the age of eight, we are like sponges, soaking up every little thing around us, whether positive or negative. This means that *everyone* develops beliefs from early childhood.

And I'm not talking about our beliefs in Father Christmas and the Tooth Fairy here (which are totally valid and real of course!). Instead, I'm talking about all the general observations we make as children that, without us even realizing, turn into our core beliefs in adult life – about who we are, what the world is like and what it has to offer us.

These childhood observations can be anything from our environment, the experiences we have, the people we meet, the things we are told, the events that unfold and the things we witness. The problem is that, as children, we don't yet have the capacity to fully process a lot of what we see, feel and experience.

Think about it: have you ever looked back at something you believed as a child and laughed at how you ever thought it to be true? I was absolutely convinced, for example, that my eyes would go square, like the television, if I sat too close to it. I also thought that if you ate the seeds of an apple, then an apple tree would grow in your stomach! I now realize, of course, that my Mum would tell me this about the TV in order to have me sit further away from it, and I'm pretty sure it was someone in the playground who told me the apple tree thing. But as a child, if you have nothing or nobody else to tell you these things *aren't* true, you have no reason to question them! So these beliefs become your truth.

A friend once relayed a story to me about his seven-year-old nephew who was convinced he could fly. I am talking full-blown convinced that, if he really wanted to, he would be able to do it. When asked what made him believe this to be *true*, considering he hadn't actually flown (obviously), he hadn't witnessed any other human fly and he didn't have wings, he simply answered, "Because Reuben at school said I could – so why *couldn't* I?"

Needless to say that, after a jump or two off a bunk bed (no *major* injuries thankfully), he realized that he couldn't, in fact, fly. And, as a teenager, he is now well aware of this downfall in the creation of humans.

The point I'm making here is that as a child you have no reason to disbelieve *anything* you are told, see or learn in any other way. And this doesn't just apply to quirky things that your parents tell you – like eating carrots will make you see in the dark or that if you swallow chewing gum it will stay in your body for seven years (honestly, who made these up!?)

With many of these random beliefs we will, of course, eventually grow up and "unlearn" them (although I still don't swallow chewing gum, just in case). But there are countless other more subtle things that we unknowingly absorb as children, and that (whether we are aware of it or not) we don't grow out of believing. And it is these that create our *core beliefs* about ourselves and the world around us.

Some of these beliefs will be positive ones that have a beneficial impact on our adult lives. But when core beliefs develop that are negative, or do not serve a useful long-term purpose in our life, they are referred to as "limiting beliefs" (given that they are likely to "limit" us from fulfilling our true potential). Unlike finding out the Tooth Fairy isn't real when you catch your parents trying to pop a coin or two under your pillow (or when you break your arm jumping off the top bunk in your attempt to fly!), we often don't just grow out of limiting beliefs. Instead, they tend to become the foundation of why we don't feel worthy – whether of love, wealth, "success", happiness or whatever else we dream of.

Now, I'm not going to try to explain the full psychology behind this here because I haven't got those skills (not a limiting belief – just a fact). But there is a lot of research out there these days about just how stuck in our *subconscious* minds our limiting beliefs are, which means that they dictate an alarming amount of our lives without us even ever knowing – unless, that is, we bring our attention to them, as I'm encouraging you to do in this chapter.

The best analogy I have ever come across to describe the difference between the conscious and subconscious mind is that the conscious mind is like our desktop – the info that is kept ready, open and accessible all the time; while the subconscious mind is like the "cloud" – storing a lot of "background" info up there, somewhere "hidden". So it's interesting that it's the *subconscious* mind that rules a lot of how we think, feel and behave!

EXPLORING THE FORMATION OF OUR LIMITING BELIEFS

In this section, I'm going to dig into where some of my own core limiting beliefs came from – in the hope that it'll make you consider some of your own "stuff" along the way. As, although your childhood may have looked different to mine, you may still have experienced some of the same things I did or find at least some similarities in the beliefs you picked up.

So, while reading this section, have a think about your *own* history, your *own* story – and see if you can identify any of your *own* limiting beliefs and when they were formed.

I grew up in North London, UK, with my Mum and my younger brother, Jordan. It was just the three of us, so we were pretty tight. And, for the most part, my childhood was pretty good.

We lived in a cosy two-bedroom flat on the second floor of a block of flats in a council estate. And everyone in our community treated each other like family. It was diverse, vibrant, friendly and everything you could have wished for in a neighbourhood. There were six blocks that created a little square, and everyone within those walls knew each other, watched each other's children, and supported one another with food or anything else when needed. All of us kids were friends, and we would spend our summers playing neighbourhood street games until the streetlights came on.

Everyone knew us, and everyone knew my mum, Elaine. She was known for being the Mum who was always singing, organizing mass trips to the park and handing out ice lollies. She was also known as the Mum who made me and my brother wear plastic grocery bags as swimwear one summer because she was sick of us getting our clothes wet in water fights! However, I came to realize that outside of our community bubble, people who didn't know us didn't think I belonged to her. This wasn't something I assumed or overheard incorrectly. I would constantly be asked, "But is she *really* your Mum? Because she is Black, and you're not."

To provide context, I'm a fair-skinned, mixed-race woman with blondish-brown hair, blue eyes and a face covered in freckles. I was born to a Black British woman (who has Jamaican parents) and a white British man (whom I didn't meet until I was 27 – we'll come to that later). Despite the several shades of difference in our skin tone, I look a lot like my mother (and behave like her, too). But this didn't stop people asking if I was really hers.

There's often a weird fascination with racial ambiguity – especially when encountered in children. The countless questions of "Where are you from? ... No really, like, where are you *from, from?*" started before I was old enough to respond, and continued throughout my childhood. And it still happens to this day!

As an adult, I've learned to simply explain that I'm from London and continue to answer "London" until the person realizes that there will be no other answer. Or, if I'm feeling particularly patient (rare!), I will use it as an opportunity to educate the person as to why it's offensive to ask. I have learned to understand the micro-aggressions behind the questioning, and the weird fascination about my heritage. But as a child it left me constantly wondering where I belonged – and if I really belonged *anywhere*.

When we meet people, whether we know it or not, we tend to make assumptions about them based on what they look like – their ethnic background, gender, age, clothes, body size or whatever else. And we tend to unknowingly form quite a fixed idea of what we "expect" from them based on these factors (which are all created by the narratives of people we already have in our minds). This is more commonly known as a stereotype – a type of bias that nobody wants to admit they have but that most people *do* have. As the incredible equality and human rights activist Femi Otitoju says, "If you have a brain, you have a bias."

When people are unable to "place" you in one of the fixed boxes in their mind, they find it difficult to create the quick-fire assumptions that dictate how to behave toward you. And this can, in turn, cause a confusion that, whether spoken or not, can make you feel uncomfortable, unseen and just bloody awkward.

When people used to ask me, as a little girl, where I was from or even, "What are you?", I remember feeling so confused. If it wasn't an innocent child at school asking me where my Mummy was in the playground and not understanding why I was pointing to a Black woman, it was a woman in our local store taking my hand and walking me to a customer service desk as a lost child, despite the fact that I had been standing right near my Mum at the time!

These early encounters were not as rare as you would hope. And, no matter how often they happened or how many times people asked me, they still stung every time because it felt like my very existence was being called into question.

I then went to high school in a pretty affluent area, where everyone had Nike drawstring bags and Gap jumpers (these were top notch designer brands to me at the time). And, while I appreciate they were just clothes, they were yet another thing that made me feel like I didn't quite belong – as my Hi-tech trainers were *not* the "in" shoe!

As the feelings of not belonging heightened, I began to internalize them.

Everyone else seemed to belong somewhere! *They* looked like their parents and other family members. There were no questions about *their* ethnic background. *They* seemed to have more in common with each other. *They* had more money than me. And *they* looked like they just "fitted".

While I had a solid group of friends, and, thankfully, I never had issues socializing (my love of MTV music videos and Spice Girls ensured this), I still couldn't shake the fact that I just didn't feel like everyone else. And that made me struggle with how I identified.

Everything that I had witnessed, experienced and heard created and fed a belief in me that I just wasn't good enough to belong *anywhere*. Not white enough. Not Black enough. Not beautiful enough. Not slim enough. Not rich enough. The list went on...

Writing this now, comfortable in the knowledge that I belong absolutely *anywhere* that I want there to be space for me, I feel sad that my feelings of not belonging were so entrenched at that time – that these encounters over the years had woven themselves into such a patchwork of negative beliefs about who I was or wasn't, what I was or wasn't capable of, and what I was or wasn't deserving of.

The patchwork had become a huge emotional blanket that I threw right over my life to try to hide myself – and it was weighing me down.

RECOGNIZING LIMITING BELIEFS IN ACTION

In order to create positive change in any areas of your life that you're not happy with, you first need to *identify* the areas in which you're feeling stuck; then *recognize* and *reframe* the limiting beliefs linked to these areas; and only *then* can you move forward.

Think for a moment about whether there are any particular areas of *your* life where you're struggling. Try not to *overthink*: what comes to mind straightaway?

Some of the most common areas are:

- Love and relationships
- Finances
- Career and work

You may feel that you aren't getting things "right" in one or two of these areas, in all of these areas, or more!

When I started this process, I felt that the areas of *my* life in need of most serious refurb were my love life and my finances (both of which felt entirely out of control!).

But it will be different for everyone at different times.

So, whatever your current situation, it's important to know that:

- Limiting beliefs are personal to you, so are likely to play out differently in *your* life from in mine.
- There will always be other people experiencing *something* similar to you though, so you are never alone, even if it may not feel like it right now.
- Limiting beliefs will trickle into your life in various ways. Some might go unnoticed for years; some might be really obvious. But looking for recurring *patterns* of unhelpful behaviours will help you to identify them and track them back to their roots.

- There are many ways in which you can begin to let go of your old beliefs and related patterns of behaviour; I hope these will become apparent as you move through the rest of the book.

For a while I couldn't connect all the dots between my failing finances, my failing relationships, other areas of my life that weren't going that well, and my old limiting beliefs. Some links were straightforward but others took me a while to grasp.

The journey of discovery involved a lot of journalling: writing things down to be able to physically see on paper what was what; then matching everything up like a strange game of Snap! There was also a lot of talking to people who were already at the *other* end of their journey to self-acceptance – to see if I could spot common patterns. And, perhaps most importantly, there was a lot of brutal honesty with myself, which was essential for me to be able to keep making breakthroughs.

As I began to gradually make the connections, I realized that in order for me to change the not-so-great areas of my life, I needed to change what I believed about myself at the very core.

Love & Relationships

Love and relationships: an area of life that is so important when it comes to our sense of self-worth and self-confidence.

On starting to really look at my past romantic relationships and how they might relate to long-held beliefs that were no longer serving me (and that I now wanted to dismantle), I realized that I had been choosing the same types of partners over and over again yet expecting the outcome to be different.

I was in a constant cycle of running headfirst into a relationship, giving so much of myself, and then feeling completely crushed – and blaming myself – when it all fell apart. I knew that I was "settling" for people and for situations that were never going to be good for me in the long term, but why?

This is not an uncommon story, so it might well be one that resonates with you. It seems to be a journey that a lot of us go on if we try to navigate relationships before we've done a lot of *inner* work on ourselves. As a result, we hang all our worth on our *external* relationships in the hope of being validated by someone else.

The game changer for me in this scenario was when I finally admitted to myself that, deep down, I was "settling" because I never felt like I *deserved* true love and contentment as a result of never feeling like I was "enough".

Only once I had been honest enough to make this sad admission was I able to start actually *changing* this belief. And only *then* was I able to finally connect with people who were good for me – stepping into relationships that were healthy, happy and balanced.

Finances

As I started to look more closely at my financial problems, I recognized the link to the belief that had developed during my childhood around not "belonging" anywhere. It suddenly made complete sense that things like my overspending, the debt I had got myself into and the constant need to have more "stuff" actually stemmed from the sense of lack that I had soaked up as a child – which was now pouring out into my adult life.

I mentioned before that my school was in a pretty affluent area and that my concept of wealth became tied up with brand names, associating "posher" brands with people who were "better than". This meant that from my early teens I began to value money and material things over anything else.

While this sounds pretty normal for many in their teenage years, for me it wasn't just about having the latest trainers. It defined how I felt about myself as well as about others. Experiencing life in the way I had, my naïve understanding was that if you had "stuff" it was because you had money, and if you had money, you were *worth something*. I thought this belief would naturally shift as I grew older – because with age, apparently, comes wisdom – but, while I did finally manage to unpack and heal this portion of my life, I was shocked at just how much it subconsciously controlled my life for so long.

I had created so much insecurity and shame around what I looked like, how I dressed and how I was living, that even though my career aspirations changed weekly, the only thing that *really* felt like it mattered to me was to earn good money, because that meant, "I would be important – and happy!"

This limiting belief caused a lot of mixed emotions as regards to what money could do in my life. I wanted it but I feared it. I felt guilt about wanting it, but I felt immense shame at not having enough of it. These emotional ties meant that I would often override practical thoughts about managing money as I couldn't get past the feeling of just wanting to be like everyone else by having "enough".

Part of the issue for me was that I was more focused on not *looking* broke than actually not *being* broke. I now realize that this was because my worth was tied up in how other people *perceived* me. I wanted people to *see* that I could afford nice things. Then they would know that I was "someone" and I could feel validated.

But this wasn't because of what anyone *else* had said they needed to see from me. It was just the way that I *myself* had perceived the world, and I therefore presumed others perceived it that way too!

This constant search for external validation meant that I ended up tens of thousands of pounds of debt. And – shock, horror – although I owned loads of "stuff", none of it had filled the void of feeling that I wasn't good enough!

Career & Work

It's common for many of us to have limiting beliefs around our career and work, whether we feel that we're not good enough for a promotion or new role that we want, or we lack confidence in what we're *already* doing. These thoughts can stem from moments where we were undermined in our childhood or be learned from poor experiences within the workplace as an adult.

If we do ever get to a point where we manage to move into a new role or get offered a great opportunity, we may take it but can then be hit with imposter syndrome – where you don't feel like you belong as you're convinced that others don't believe you are qualified, competent or experienced enough. With this comes the feeling that you're going to be exposed as a fraud, which causes you to work like mad in order to hide the "truth" from everyone else. A fruitless task that is truly exhausting!

Thoughts associated with work-related limiting beliefs can often sound something like this:

- "I don't have what it takes."
- "I'm not smart or talented enough."
- "I'd never be lucky enough to get an opportunity like that."
- "There's no point in trying for that promotion, as someone else will get it."

I have experienced such thoughts countless times throughout my career – and even while writing this book. Sometimes you just feel so overwhelmed that you want to quit so that you don't embarrass yourself. However, I have learned – both in my personal life and in my professional life in recruitment (an area that I have now worked in for over a decade) – that opportunities like job offers, promotions and all the rest don't generally just land on your lap. They aren't just handed to anyone and don't happen by chance. Learning to truly accept that you *deserve* to be where you are and that you are *worthy* of any success that comes your way is key.

THE GOOD NEWS ABOUT LIMITING BELIEFS

It's pretty clear by now just how much of a role limiting beliefs play in how we live our lives. They literally limit life – by limiting possibilities and limiting happiness.

But the great news about any beliefs that we hold is that, while they may *feel* like facts and rock-solid truths, they actually aren't! (Remember the flying seven-year-old?) On the contrary, beliefs are not fixed, even though some of them might have been engrained in us for years. As such, we are able to dismantle old ones once we become aware of them. And we can then create new ones – changing our mindset from limit*ing* to limit*less*.

UNSUBSCRIBING FROM LIMITING BELIEFS

Have you ever tried to unsubscribe from an email? You probably initially subscribed to get some updates a while ago and you now keep getting a host of unwanted emails. Sometimes it's super easy to unsubscribe – one click and you never hear from them again; other times, the directions are hidden at the bottom of the email in a font size that would be small even to an ant, and you have to click through, scroll down, click again, scroll up, type a reason, provide them with the DNA of your firstborn and a sacrificial lamb, and only *then* can you unsubscribe.

Unsubscribing from the limiting negative beliefs that you hold about yourself can feel a bit like this. Some beliefs will feel pretty easy to overcome – you are able to quickly identify the source of them, recognize the impact they are having, and switch your behaviour to accommodate a new, more positive way of thinking.

There will then be other beliefs that are really *not* so easy to move away from. They will be complicated and take more time to identify, process and unlearn. But don't worry – there will never be any requirements for your DNA or a sacrificial lamb! And it is *always* worth taking the time to unsubscribe from *any* idea that tells you you're not good enough! It might take a bit of time, but remember: small, consistent choices all add up.

So, now for the big question: how do you move forward from here? How do you even begin to unlearn things that are etched into your mind and take up space without you even really thinking about it? Well, once you have *identified* that these beliefs are there and you want to unsubscribe from them, the next step is to *reframe* them ...

REFRAMING LIMITING BELIEFS

When I started researching my limiting beliefs and wanted to take action to start the Great Un-learn, I came across a brilliant set of questions and statements in a journal gift from a friend, which really helped me to understand what my core beliefs were. Up until then, I had no idea the specifics of my beliefs because I had just lived life without really delving into why I felt the way I did about things.

Having issues with "feeling like I didn't belong" meant that I had borrowed, learned and adopted so many limiting beliefs from *other* people that I couldn't really have told you what I thought or felt for *myself*. So, I started writing them down to try to get some clarity. I wrote the following headers at the top of a page:

- I am ...
- Life is ...
- People are ...

And I then went about finishing each of these sentences time and time again. Here are examples that featured in what I wrote:

- *I am not capable*
- *Life is hard*
- *People are untrustworthy*

- *I am alone*
- *Life is complicated*
- *People are unloving*

Pretty heavy and self-limiting, eh?

I kept writing and writing – until I felt like I had spilled both my entire heart and my entire brain onto the page and ta da! Just like that, I had emptied my mind of my limiting beliefs, right? Now they were down on paper, I would be free of them, yes?

It's obviously not *quite* that simple! BUT being able to see and accept the patterns in my statements was a great starting point from which to start unsubscribing from them one at a time and then reframing them as lighter, more positive and liberating beliefs that could be newly subscribed to!

The process of reframing the beliefs tends to look like this for me:

Gather Evidence Against the Old Belief

Scour your brain for real-life examples that disprove the limiting belief. For example, if addressing the belief "I am not capable", I would think of as many things as possible that I once thought I *wasn't* capable of but that I then went on to achieve, such as being offered a dream job, passing an exam that I thought was above my level, or showing up when I didn't think I could.

Ask "What If?"

Ask what the potential outcome would be if you reframed the limiting belief in hand. For example, if I *didn't* believe that "Life is hard", how would I feel? In this case, I would feel happier, lighter and more able because I wouldn't feel the pressure of things being so difficult. I would also move forward with more ease from any situations dragging me down. And who wouldn't want *that*?

Ask "Does my Belief about 'People' Apply to Everyone?"

Ask yourself if your belief about "people" can really be universal. This can often make you realize that your thinking is lacking in logic. For example, can *all* people *really* be "untrustworthy"? No! Otherwise nobody would have good relationships, and nobody would do anything or go anywhere! Yes, logically there are *some* untrustworthy people (and you may have encountered a few of them in your time). But it can't apply to everyone – hence debunking another of your negative beliefs.

Track Positive Change

One of the best ways to keep up momentum with reframing limiting beliefs is by writing down all the times you have a more positive thought process or outcome as a result of this self-development work that you are doing! You are your own best case study, and you will find it easier to keep making change when you see the first-hand evidence of progress for yourself.

Set Up a New Set of Replacement Beliefs

It's time to grab a fresh piece of paper and write the same three headings as before:

- I am ...
- Life is
- People are ...

But this time write a long list of how you would *like* to think and feel about yourself, life and other people if there was nothing standing in your way, and if anything was possible (which it is!). Things that feel like the opposite of your old limiting beliefs.

For example, among the positive replacement beliefs that I wrote at this stage were:

- *I am beautiful*
- *Life is abundant*
- *People are kind*

- *I am a respected senior manager*
- *Life is good*
- *People are forgiving*

Keep writing until your pages are full of all the wonderful things that you would like to be, see and feel.

And the next step is then to actually stop believing the statements from your first page of statements, and start wholeheartedly believing in, and acting on, these new aspirational statements ...

FOCUSING ON THE POSITIVE

When we were kids, my brother and I used to play a game during car journeys that involved us looking out for specific car colours and registrations. My Mum would say "red cars" or "X reg", for example, and every time we saw a car that fitted the bill, we would have to shout out. It kept us entertained for hours, as we would get completely lost in focusing to make sure we didn't miss one.

When we got to the end of the journey, she would ask if we had seen cars in any other colours, for example black cars, and we would swear blind that we hadn't seen a single one. Realistically, of course, there would have been countless black cars on the road, but the point is that we weren't looking for them, so in our minds, there just weren't any.

Similarly, the feelings you hold about yourself – whether positive or negative – only exist if you look for them and if you focus on them. So if, for example, you tell yourself something negative about the way you do something, the way you look, or a comment that someone has made to you, you will start to see this negativity in *everything*. And you will likely even try to use it as evidence against yourself – to confirm that your existing limiting beliefs about yourself are true!

When you are in a negative mindset and that's all you can see, then it is all you will feel, too. Anything outside of that will feel unobtainable. You will only start to notice and believe the *positive* things if you make a choice to shut off the negative voice and switch your focus *completely* to the positive.

I use this process all the time. If, for example, I'm having a day where I feel bad about myself, or just woke up on the wrong side of the bed, I give myself a moment to refocus. During this time, I zoom in on the things that I *love* about my personality, the things I am blessed with, the parts of me that make me feel safe and comfortable, the goodness that may happen (or may have already happened) that day, and I focus on them and them *only*.

I implore you to give yourself moments, hours and days where you don't seek to notice any negative. I know what you're thinking: you don't "seek" them purposely *now* – but to some degree we *do*.

A good example is when my husband irritates me or we've had an argument. In these moments, I don't tend to sit back trying to think of all the wonderful things he is, does and can be (which would actually be a really useful thing to do!). Instead, I torture myself by thinking of all the *other* times he has annoyed me or we have argued, and I use this to justify my frustration! I don't do this on purpose; it's just a habit based on my old limiting patterns.

This negative-to-positive mindset switch can be applied to almost any area of our lives, but can be particularly helpful when we think about *ourselves*. You are never going to see anything good or have the capability to use positive thoughts as evidence to affirm *goodness* in yourself if you don't make a concerted effort to look for the positives. Your energy goes where your attention flows, and right now all your energy is likely being spent on believing your old negative thoughts.

"I am not good enough" was a limiting belief I held for years. And because I was so adamant that it was true, I was convinced that it was the reason that anything and everything went wrong in my life. If I didn't get a job, it was because I wasn't good enough. If I didn't get the guy, it was because I wasn't good enough. If I gained yet another pound – you guessed it! – it was because I wasn't good enough.

I never even considered that there could be *other* reasons for any of those outcomes simply because I wasn't *looking* for any other reasons. My brain would tell me by default that *this* was the reason.

It was only by embarking on the journey to *change* my beliefs that I even became *aware* that there were other possible factors, circumstances and people involved that I had no control over – such as a boss who projected her insecurities on to me, and an ex who also had insecurity issues. In fact, there were *lots* of factors evidencing that not *everything* was because I wasn't good enough. And, in many cases, it wasn't about me *at all*.

So, how do you *stop* focusing on the loud, negative beliefs and *actively start* listening to the quieter positive voices instead?

One of the key strategies is to learn to show yourself compassion and empathy each day – feelings we often seem to reserve only for *other* people; this will be covered in more detail in Chapter 3. Without self-compassion, we are fighting a losing battle, likely to never overcome the constant barrage of negative limits that we place on ourselves.

A friend once didn't get a job that she had really wanted and was very upset about it. Knowing her well, I knew she was good enough to have got it. In fact, I knew that she was *more than* good enough, and it was their loss for not taking her on. I was giving her the good friend pep talk by telling her exactly this when she replied, "I wish I could tell that to myself!" And I wished she was able to do this, too. But I also knew that, at that time, I wouldn't have been able to give myself that pep talk either – and that I therefore needed to make a change for myself. Often the kind, reassuring way that we are able talk to our friends is so contradictory to the way that we treat ourselves!

The fantastic thing about all this is that once you start having days where you *aren't* so negative toward yourself, or where you're kind to yourself and actually feel fabulous, you'll start seeing just what an enormous impact being more positive to yourself can truly have on the level of joy that you tend to experience in everyday life.

Owning It Top Tip

Start and end each day by thinking of something that you are grateful for. As you become more confident in this, add more things to both your morning and evening list. Be sure to include things about yourself, as well as about external things in your life.

BECOMING "LIMITLESS"

My husband Trevor once convinced me to watch a movie that he had chosen. We have totally different ideas of what constitutes a good movie but I gave it a try and it turns out that movie, while not my favourite ever, was life-changing due to the conversation that it led to.

It was about a guy called Eddie who's down on his luck in life when he comes across a drug that transforms his mind from being limited (and limiting) to razor sharp. As a result, he suddenly transforms his life and his career (he's a stockbroker). The stock market grows exponentially, meaning he becomes mega rich and successful ... and then some people want to capture him and it gets a bit dark. But, I mean, don't worry about that bit – it's not relevant.

Anyway, years later, I still remember the discussion that Trevor and I had when we'd finished watching it. We started discussing all the things we would do if we were "limitless" – with the power to unlock something in our brain that meant we could transform *anything* about our lives. We talked about travelling, building businesses, growing our family, buying nice things, supporting our parents, and having a lavish house with a private chef! While there is obviously no special medicine that does this, and the movie is completely fictional, the message of breaking down limiting beliefs in order to transform life really stuck with me. And the idea of unlocking your caged mind by unsubscribing from your limiting beliefs is central to this.

Think about what you would do if you could click your fingers and have no barriers or other opinions to stop you. You could be and do anything you wanted. Imagine exactly what that life would be like. What would your morning routine be as you woke up each day? What would you do for work? If you chose to be in a relationship, what would that relationship feel like? What would you wear? What time would you go to bed at night? Think about all the tiny details of what this dream life would be like.

If I then told you that all of the above was *well* within your reach – just on the other side of your limiting beliefs – would you start making a change? I hope so …

Self-Reflection Questions

On Breaking Free of Limiting Beliefs

- What are my key limiting beliefs? (I am …/Life is …/ People are …)
- What would I *like* to believe and feel? (I am …/Life is …/ People are …)
- What are things that I see in others that make me feel scared in my own life?
- What are my common excuses for not having, doing or being the things I desire in life?
- What could happen if I let go of, and reframe, the limiting beliefs that I'm learning to identify?

GUIDED TASK
Write a Letter to Your Younger Self

Often, when looking back at our childhood and exploring where our limiting beliefs started, there are many things we wish we could tell our younger selves – as a means of guidance and/or reassurance. This activity allows you to do just this. When I started doing this exercise on the advice of my therapist, I'd often find myself giving warnings of the things to come, or positively intervening at the points where I now realize that certain limiting beliefs were established. Although I have now written many letters like this over the years, I know there are still many more to come, as I find it such a valuable exercise.

Why Write This Letter?

Writing a letter to your younger self is a great tool to identify some of the key moments in life where your limiting beliefs were formed. Going back in time and really "seeing" the person you were then can also begin a journey of self-acceptance and healing, by allowing you to show yourself the kindness and empathy that you may have needed at the time but didn't get. It is also a great opportunity for forgiving both yourself and others for things in the past, for letting go of feelings that no longer serve you, and for moving on.

How to Write Such a Letter

Just write! There's no right or wrong here. Don't worry if you're not mad keen on writing; the letter doesn't have to be *War and Peace* (although there's no restriction on length either). Nobody but you is going to see what you write (unless you want them to), so be honest. Is there something in particular that you would like to say to your younger self, or a particular event that you would like to address and get healing from? Think of it like writing a diary entry, and try not to put too much pressure on yourself. You can do this! Once you've written it, do whatever feels right with the letter – tuck it away in a drawer, pop it in a memory box or even frame it! It's entirely up to you.

Here's an example letter that I wrote to myself:

JESS! I wish you knew how much you are going to overcome. You're totally confused now and seeking validation from all sorts of places (some better looking than others!). But there will come a point in time when all those feelings of self-doubt and wondering why you're not good enough will have passed, and the validation and love that you are searching for everywhere else you will find in the most beautiful person: you.

Things will get worse before they get better. I know that's crap, but it's the way the world works sometimes. Just know that coming out the other side is EPIC.

"Hope" isn't a word you use much right now; it's not one you think you deserve. But you do deserve it and it will show up in your life in so many ways. You just have to keep your eyes open to be able to see it.

Just keep swimming Jess. Just keep swimming …

And eat the bloody cake. All of it. Not just a stupid slice.

Girl, just eat.

GUIDED TASK
Out with the Old, In with the New

This is an activity that has helped me time and time again when I've needed to get more clarity on what I want, feel more positive in myself and let go of limiting beliefs in my life that no longer serve me. There's just so much power in writing things down, as it somehow makes thoughts and ideas seem so much more real and tangible.

What You Will Need

- Two pieces of paper
- A pen
- Yourself (obviously)

What To Do

1. Write down on your first piece of paper as many things as you can think of that have stopped you from doing things you have wanted to do in life – and that continue to put a pause on your dreams, a dampener on your life and stop you from Owning It!

   This step can feel tough, as when you begin to break down all the things that have been holding you back in different ways, it can make you feel frustrated, sad, irritated and maybe even angry. Try not to judge yourself though, as your feelings are valid, whatever they are.

   And remember: it's you and you alone who is going to see what you write down, so be as candid as possible.

   Here's an example of one of my lists:

   - What other people might say
   - I am not beautiful enough
   - I need to lose more weight

- I am not a good enough person
- I don't really deserve it

2. Now take your second piece of paper and write down a list of things that you would love to do, feel, see, experience, achieve or whatever else as you move forward in life – your very own wish list, if you like.

These can be anything your heart desires; there's nothing too big or too small. So there's no need to hold back. This list is all about *you* and what you want to feel and be. So, whatever that might be, just write it down here.

Here's an example of one of my lists:

- Wear that red dress
- Feel sexy
- Speak up at meetings
- Ask for a raise at work
- Become self-employed

3. Revisit your first list (of things that have been holding you back) and get rid of it! I have a fire that I usually burn mine in! If you choose to burn yours, too, be sure to choose somewhere safe. However, you don't need to burn it. You can rip it up, shred it, or do a Carole Baskin and feed it to the tigers! (Actually, on

second thoughts, maybe best not take that route!) The point is that it really doesn't matter how you get rid of it. The important thing is that you do get rid of it – and therefore symbolically let go of all the things that have been getting in the way of you living the truly contented, fulfilled life that you deserve.

This is your chance to let go of all your old self-limiting beliefs and make space for more feelings of hope, joy, confidence and love.

If you need to drink some wine, dance around, swear or anything else to help you let things go, then go for it! (All done responsibly, of course!)

4. Now, just sit quietly. Breathe deeply. And allow yourself to notice any little butterflies of excitement about all the wonderful things that you have just made space for – and that are now to come. Allow yourself to really feel into any such flutterings of excitement, because you deserve to!

You are in control of your life now. You are worthy of the freedom that is going to come into your life. You are beautiful, you are awesome and you are an absolute badass!

Chapter 2

Finding & Stepping into Your Inner Confidence

When I think of the concept of confidence – and stepping into it in a liberated way – I find myself thinking of drag queens. To me, they are the epitome of confidence and power – as well as having *all* the glam, of course! Ru Paul has led the way for many, and has been very open about how becoming the icon that he has on the drag scene has allowed him to truly fall in love with the person he is today. He once said, "To limit yourself to one thing, it's your business. But you have a choice." And it's true – you *do* have a choice – to become whoever or whatever you want to be.

The term alter ego – which, by dictionary definition, means "alternative self" – derives from the Latin meaning "other I". A lot of celebrities have an "other I" that they embody when on stage. Some of the most famous include David Bowie/ Ziggy Stardust, Marshall Mathers/Eminem, Beyoncé/Sasha Fierce – and, if you're a '90s kid (like me), you'll also know Miley Cyrus/Hannah Montana. Taking on a bold character like this can create a bridge between the person that you "normally" are and the person that you *want* to be, giving you freedom to behave in more creative, and sometimes even more authentic, ways than how you might usually be perceived.

In May 2014 – when I was being bullied at work, on a Ross and Rachel "break" from my husband Trevor, and trying to work out how to potty train a small human – my own "alternative self" was born when I created a website on WordPress under the moniker "The Fat Funny One". I had been telling a friend a story on the phone to help her through a hard time, and she told me that *everyone* needed to hear what I had to say! She suggested that I start a blog to get my stories out there, under a pseudonym if I didn't want to "own them" under my own name (oh, the irony!). So that is what I did!

I already had an Instagram page in my own name, but that had essentially just been a weight loss diary. So I changed the name to The Fat Funny One and slowly changed the emphasis to be more about my confidence journey and being happy to take *up* space in the world, rather than trying to make myself smaller! If I'm honest, I didn't have aspirations for it to be anything other than a place where I could just be myself and maybe make a few people laugh with random stories, funny quips and some brutal honesty about the highs and lows of learning to love yourself. So, with the help of some random images from Google to give it a bit of life, I took to the keyboard and just started to write …

While on the inside I was questioning my very existence and wondering what my next move would be, I had, without quite knowing what I was doing, created an online alter ego through which I could share stories, be funny and have a creative outlet that let me forget about what was going on in my reality! The Fat Funny One gave me this little pocket of online joy and freedom!

I had no following, of course, but I began sharing my blog posts on my personal Facebook page with friends and family, and asked them to share it. The first time I did it my stomach was in absolute knots. I was petrified that I would be rejected by everyone and that nobody would find it funny, entertaining or even read it, apart from my Mum (but that's a Mother's duty, of course). I thought I'd probably just end up embarrassing myself in front of a bunch of old school friends, my aunties on Facebook and a few ex-colleagues.

While I wasn't *hiding* behind the persona because I wasn't anonymous (although at times down the line I wished I was), creating The Fat Funny One allowed me to obtain a level of confidence that I otherwise don't think I could have "owned".

The persona gave me the opportunity to "fake it till I make it". I was projecting a confidence to the outside world that, as "Jess", I definitely didn't have at the time. I just hoped that if I did it for long enough that maybe some of it would seep into my reality and stick.

But what I didn't realize was that creating the platform in the first place had taken a lot of courage – so was this courage a form of confidence in itself?

GROWING CONFIDENCE
THROUGH COURAGE

I never really thought there was a difference between confidence and courage. I just thought they were different words for the same kind of thing. It was only on listening one day to *The 5 Second Rule* by US motivational speaker and author Mel Robbins (a legit epic who I cannot recommend highly enough!) that I realized there was a big difference between the two (although they often work hand in hand).

She described confidence as having faith in yourself – doing small things that affirm you are good at something or that you have the ability to do it in the first place; and described courage as a driving force within you – an innate quality that will give you the strength to do something even if you feel scared, or haven't got the confidence that there will be a positive outcome.

There's a misconception out there that you are either born with confidence or you are not – that it's just part of your personality. But I don't buy into that. I believe that confidence is a skill that can be developed and grown – and that can also ebb and flow over time depending on life events that affect how you feel.

When I hear my Mum and others describe what I was like when I was little, it makes me realize that I was a pretty confident child. However, as I grew older – and my limiting beliefs (see Chapter 1) started creeping in and getting louder – this confidence shrank, and I stopped being, or becoming, the person I really wanted to be.

I see *now* that this is because confidence generally grows from – or is built on – feelings of acceptance, belonging, self-trust and wellbeing. And, given that I had struggled to feel those things as I grew up, it was hard to continue to *grow* in confidence until I made the conscious choice to actively work on getting to know, accept and trust my authentic self – and really Own my life. This choice really is one of the best investments that I've ever made – and that I continue to make every day.

Another example of ebbing and flowing confidence in my life can be seen in my relationship with driving. I was generally always described as a "confident driver", and, for the most part, I was. I felt like I was solid, responsible and safe. And I had the confidence to drive wherever, whenever – until one day I had an accident. The accident "knocked my confidence" and made me question my driving ability. It took me quite a while to rebuild that faith in myself – and to accept that the accident wasn't even my fault, as it happened.

But, interestingly, while my confidence was out of the picture, it was my courage (as well as the fact that I had to get to work!) that got me back in the car again and slowly allowed me to regain my confidence.

While there are differences between confidence and courage, one is not better than the other, and there is certainly no perfect balance between them that we're "meant to" have. The important thing is that, whether or not you *feel* confident or courageous, you have within you the capacity to be either or both of these things at any time! It's just about bringing them to the surface.

So take a moment now and again to reflect on situations in the past in which you have shown confidence and/or courage –

and really feel into this to remind yourself just how much you're already capable of!

LEARNING TO NAVIGATE BOTH THE SNAKES AND LADDERS OF LIFE

Low confidence tends to manifest in different ways for different people. But the common theme, regardless of how it shows up in your life, is that *it will* hold you back.

The good news, however, is that – whether you're lacking in confidence about how you look, things that you've done, things that you've not yet done, or any of the other endless ways in which you can doubt yourself – there is a way to *change* how you feel.

Your relationship with confidence as you travel through life can sometimes feel like playing a game of Snakes and Ladders. One moment, you can feel like you're doing really well, building yourself up, growing in confidence and moving up those ladders. Yet, just a few more rolls of the dice of life and you might land on a snake – whether in the form of a negative comment from someone, a down day (where you just can't shake off feeling bad), a rejection of some sort, or whatever else. Just like that, after climbing up all those ladders (and building your confidence), you slip down to the bottom and have to start the building process again.

It can feel like being on an exhausting emotional rollercoaster! And it's one that I spent years and years on. I often just wanted to give up as, despite enjoying the highs of the ladders, I just didn't want to continue feeling the levels of disappointment and hurt that I did every time I "landed on a snake".

Both the "snakes" and "ladders "of life come in various shapes and sizes so will all affect you differently. Some may have very little effect and pass quickly, while others may have a dramatic and long-lasting effect. Some may even end up becoming a fundamental part of who you are – part of your belief system and the way you see the world.

One day, after my gazillionth tumble down what seemed like a particularly long snake – and in despair about the frequency of the snakes I was encountering – I came to the realization that the game of life isn't about waiting until you meet *no* snakes on your journey (there will always be snakes of some kind or another given we can't control external circumstances). Rather, it's about how you let the snakes *affect* you, how far you let them drag you down, and how long it takes you to start to look for, and climb, the ladders away from them. Even when it feels like you can't do it or the ladder seems to steep, just take the first step.

You are in control of where you go (and how quickly) – and crashing down, defeated each time, is no longer an option. Personally, I realized that the biggest snakes in my life were my limiting beliefs (which we looked at in the previous chapter) as well as the negative opinions of others (which we'll discuss in Chapter 4). But it's up to *you* to figure out what the most draining and deadly "snakes" in your *own* life are – and what ladders will help you keep rising above these (see the GUIDED TASK at the end of this chapter, to help you with this).

In the new *Jumanji* film (the old-school original was better, but bear with me), there is a scene where the characters are faced with a black mamba snake and Kevin Hart's character instantly knows what to do to survive: "defang" the snake! There will always be ways to "defang" *your* snakes in life, too. My hope is that the guidance in this book will arm you with the tools you need to defang whatever snakes you encounter, as well as to build more ladders ...

CONFIDENCE IS CONTAGIOUS – SURROUND YOURSELF WITH POSITIVE PEOPLE

One of the first and best things I did when learning how to build my confidence was find authentic examples of other people who had already done the same. I felt that I needed to see real-life examples so that I could really believe it was possible. I wanted to find people who had found or built a lot of confidence-boosting ladders and were still climbing them, so that I could have a chance at building my own.

At first, I fixed totally on social media, focusing on people who I deemed super confident in the way they presented their content or came across on videos. But this only took me so far. As we all know, social media can become a bit of a comparison game. And it's often difficult to connect on a more personal level or get to know what is *really* happening in someone's life, behind the gloss. As a result, you can often only make assumptions from what you are shown on the surface.

So, while social media was a wonderful source of initial inspiration (I will talk more about how to manage social media in Chapter 6), I also wanted salt-of-the-earth, real-life examples. I wanted – and needed – to see people in my own life who were doing the things that I wanted to do and living the way that I wanted to live.

So I started looking ...

From colleagues at work who were great at presenting and well respected by their colleagues, to friends who were brilliant at dealing with adversity, to family members who just seemed confident in their own skin – if there was something about the way a person was that I felt I could learn from, I started reaching out and reconnecting with them.

It seems obvious now, but being around positive people who have even just *some* of the qualities that *you* would like to have, or who are doing *some* of the things that *you* would like to do, can make you feel more inspired, more willing to try new things and, ultimately, more confident.

There's a line here that can cross into feeling intimidated and overwhelmed if you're not careful, so it's important to ensure that those you're learning from lift you *up*, rather than dragging you down into any kind of comparison game (something that is so easy to fall into, and certainly something that I have fallen into a lot in the past myself!).

When I created The Fat Funny One, I never thought in a million years that I could end up becoming any kind of confidence role model for *others*, given that I didn't have any myself! The ladders I had started building through the blog were a good start, but often too short or on shaky ground, so were easy to fall off. Not to mention just how many snakes I was constantly allowing to take me down!

If you had told me then that I would now be writing a book on confidence, I would have literally laughed so hard (and so nervously!) that I would have probably accidentally farted. But here I am, writing this book – which just goes to show that confidence really *can* be nurtured and grown!

When you begin to transform your own life, you have no idea who is watching and learning from you. So it's really important that you choose, and surround yourself with, good role models.

For me, this meant that I had to really reflect on the relationships in my life. I had to do a deep dive into who I was connecting with and how they made me feel. Were they helping or hindering my progress? And were there potentially snakes among them causing me to slip and fall when I was finally starting to climb a few ladders?

Unfortunately, on doing this deep dive, I discovered there were people in my life who were deeply toxic and unhealthy for me. Quite frankly, there were some big old pythons that I needed to unwind from me as soon as possible. But how do you even begin to step back, or walk away, from people who you have known for such a long time, are close to or, in some instances, are even related too? It isn't easy, that's for sure, but let me assure you that, in the end, it's definitely worth it.

Letting go of bad relationships in order to create a healthy circle of people around you, whose awesomeness you can soak up, is a process that we will look at in more depth in Chapter 4. Be warned, however, that you will need a big ol' dose of self-love to do this. And the kicker is that you haven't yet got to the confident, fully empowered place where you need to be to do it, because said toxic connections are holding you back from getting there!

This is where courage swoops in. Confident or not, you are already courageous – if you're willing to dig in and find this aspect of yourself, of course. We all have the strength and courage inside of us to start stepping out of our "snakey" comfort zone of bad relationships and to take the first step on the ladder to a happier, more confident life. So, are you up for tapping into your inner courage and going for it?

QUICK CONFIDENCE BOOSTERS

While the road to authentic confidence is by no means straightforward, there are plenty of small but significant things that you can do for boosts along the way. Remember: it's all the small, consistent decisions that result in true long-term change! So why not try some of the following simple but effective "tricks" any time you need a lift ...

Smile

Research says that the physical act of smiling is proven to not only boost your personal mood but also to make you see the outside world and those around you more positively. Even when your smile isn't genuine, your brain is unable to tell the difference, which means your body will release chemicals that make you feel happier (our bodies are blooming awesome, eh?). I hope you're fake smiling as you read this – especially if you're on public transport!

Fake smiling can be uncomfortable and awkward at first, but it can genuinely make you feel more positive. And when you're feeling more positive, you will naturally feel more confident.

The same goes for laughing, too. If you can fake laugh a few times, you are likely to end up laughing for real. So, go on, try it! – although maybe not on public transport this time?!

Be Your Own Hype Man

The biggest superstars out there all have a hype man! This is the name traditionally given to the person, or act, that warms up a crowd before the main show. Only in your *own* life, you need to be both the hype man *and* the main act.

To get hyped is to get excited – so it's time to get excited about yourself, the things you're capable of, the opportunities awaiting you in life, and taking another step in your journey toward Owning It.

The best (and most awkward) way that I "hype" myself is literally to talk to myself as if I was the hype man (occasionally high fiving myself too). This has come in particularly useful when I've done live shows or big events where my anxiety has got the better of me and I feel drowned in self-doubt. In such moments, I give myself a pep talk to transform my anxiety into excitement! I literally look in the mirror and tell myself: "You got this. You are amazing! Do you know just *how* amazing? Oh, you are going to be so great!" And I keep going and going until I feel ready to take on the challenge – still nervous, but now courageous and, dare I say it, even confident.

Try it. Just say something nice about yourself – out loud if you can. You don't need to be looking in a mirror, but it totally helps!

There's a brilliant scene in the '90s movie *Cool Runnings* (absolute classic), where one of the athletes, Brenner, encourages the other, Junior, to look in the mirror and say affirmations to himself when he is full of self-doubt after a knock-back. Brenner tells him to shout, "I am pride! I am power! I am a badass mother who don't take no crap off of nobody!". He makes him say it several times until he is shouting it, starting to believe it and feels confident enough to go out and stand up for himself. There are countless brilliant scenes in the film, but this one has stuck with me for decades because it's a reminder to me of just how useful it can be to be your own hype man!

Even if you feel super ridiculous trying it, I'll bet it feels a damn sight better than just sticking with your otherwise incessant negative internal dialogue ...

Listen to Uplifting Music

If hyping yourself up just feels like one step too far for now, you might prefer to listen to a feel-good song that will have the same effect. I *love* a classic empowerment song such as Aretha Franklin's *Respect*, or blasting some Lizzo to remind myself that I'm "100 per cent that bitch"! I often do this in the car on the way to work when I need a boost, or when I'm getting ready to go out (even just for the school run).

Listening to the lyrics and really singing them 'til your heart's content does wonders for your soul. It's also a chance to channel any diva alter ego that may be lurking or to channel *Drag Race* lip-sync battles!

I can't tell you how many times I've caught the eye of other drivers at traffic lights as I sing my little heart out. And because

I've worked so hard to be confident in my own skin, this now makes me laugh and brings me even more joy (rather than me dying of embarrassment – as I once would have)!

Sit Up. Stand Up. Speak Up.

Often in the past, when I wasn't feeling confident, whether consciously or not, I would try and make myself smaller. I would sit at the back in meetings, talk quietly (hard to imagine this one now), and I would slouch. All of these were physical consequences of the way I was feeling inside. My lack of confidence was showing.

Consider how you are sitting right now (albeit that you're reading a book, so hopefully pretty comfy). Now consider the last time you were in a meeting, in front of others or doing something that maybe made you feel vulnerable or lacking in confidence. Were you slouching, head down? Did you stand up tall and make yourself seen? Were you raising your voice to be fully heard?

I've become so much more aware over the years of the role that my body language plays, not only in what I communicate to others but also in what I'm communicating to *myself* about how I'm feeling.

Richard Petty, a professor in Psychology at the University of Ohio co-founded a study in 2009 around how posture affects confidence.

He said in a research report: "Most of us were taught that sitting up straight gives a good impression to other people but it turns out that our posture can also affect how we think about ourselves. If you sit up straight, you end up convincing yourself that you are far more confident and powerful by the posture you're in."

We'll get on to the complex relationship you may have with your body in more detail in Chapter 5. But for now, give yourself a gift: sit up nice and straight, elongate your spine, open your chest and, if you have them, stick out your tits! Stay in this posture and see how you feel. It may feel uncomfortable and a little unnatural for you at first, but it's likely to make you feel more powerful and more confident.

This also works with standing up when you want to be seen, and speaking in a firm voice (either to yourself or others) when you want to be heard. Try it – whether you are in a room full of people, dealing with your children or even alone.

I've been using these quick confidence-boosting tools for years now and they've made a big difference. I've been using them for so long now, in fact, that they've become second nature to me, so are easy for me to do. What's harder is to know how to step into feeling more confident about things that you deem as weaknesses or flaws in yourself, so let's turn to that …

GETTING TO KNOW YOUR STRENGTHS

I've worked in recruitment for over a decade, so have carried out loads of interviews for loads of roles in loads of industries, with a wonderful variety of people. Interviews are pretty standard, and although they vary slightly depending on what you're hiring for, certain questions are commonly asked. A popular question that has never sat right with me (it feels to me like it is setting people up to fail) is: "What would you say are your strengths and weaknesses?"

The weakness part of the question often throws people. How honest should you be? Do you admit you're "bad" at something and have things about yourself that you want to "fix"? Do you answer with, "I can't actually think of anything", and just sound arrogant? It's a poorly worded question that doesn't help anyone get the best value from the situation.

I spent years cringing every time I had to ask people that question, and I have also been asked it multiple times in my own career history; you may have been, too.

A few years into my career I got the opportunity to work on a project about interview structures and processes, so I took the opportunity to look at ways that we could ask questions to get the *best* out of candidates. And this "strengths and weaknesses" question was the first on my list to look into – and hopefully reframe.

When thinking about the question honestly (not in a professional setting, where the answer is more often than not "I'm too much of a perfectionist"), how many of us are likely to have a list as long as our arm for weaknesses, yet find it pretty difficult to present our key strengths?

This realization got me thinking about how we could help steer people away from this often unhelpful focus on what they perceive as "weaknesses" or "flaws" – and move them toward really loving and Owning who they are with more authentic confidence (whether in an interview or elsewhere). Several ways to do this dawned on me:

- Focus on your strengths
- Get comfortable with *listing* your strengths
- Accept your *whole* self

Focus on Your Strengths

What if we could get candidates to focus on just what they're really good at, instead of what they're both "good" at (strengths) and "bad" at (weaknesses). The idea was that this would keep people's minds firmly on the value that they could bring to the table, rather than using up at least half their energy thinking about "weaknesses" that they needed to "fix". While there are obviously benefits in knowing that it could be useful to get better at certain things, there is a time and place for this.

So, we were excited to start asking interview candidates, "What skills do you think you *excel* at and how do you use this in your daily/work life?" The transformation in answers was mega, as it allowed people to shine in a whole different way. There is a natural growth in confidence when you begin to talk about things that you know you can do and feel good about.

Get Comfortable with *Listing* Your Strengths

Many of us (particularly females, according to research) tend to shy away from talking about the things that we are good at or have achieved. We have often been conditioned to believe that humility is such a desirable trait that we don't want to shout too loudly or positively about ourselves for fear of coming across as arrogant, rude or full of ourselves. But – in my *humble* opinion! – there's nothing wrong with being full of yourself!

The whole notion that we shouldn't big ourselves up, shout about our strengths or even boast when we have done something wonderful is just crazy to me. The more I celebrate others when they do something great, the more comfortable I become at celebrating my own achievements too.

Think about some of your best qualities and let them start going round in your head (you'll also find a GUIDED TASK at the end of this chapter, to help you with this). If nothing much comes to mind at first, consider this: if you were to be called out by someone as an expert at something, what would it be for? (And you're not allowed to say nothing!) Maybe your friends always come to you for advice or support, maybe you have an incredible physical skill or maybe you bring a certain creative spark to the table! The point here is to really think about – and make a mental list of – all the wonderful things that make you *you* – and embrace them.

Without realizing it, many of us tend to measure our strengths on a scale of *comparison* in our own heads: we only view ourselves as "good" at something if we feel we are better than others, and we view ourselves as "bad" at something if we don't feel that we do it as *well* as others. But this is unhelpful, as what other people can do is irrelevant! All you need to be concerned with when identifying and listing *your* strengths is *you!* – and the unique combination of traits and skills that only *you* can offer!

Accept Your *Whole* Self

Understanding and accepting that you are whole (and "enough") exactly as you are is so important.

There's no such thing as "perfection". We are all created differently, with different qualities, abilities and skill sets; this is what makes each of us unique and wonderful. We are all perfect in our imperfection. And this is why it's essential to love and Own *everything* about ourselves.

Sure, we *all* have things that we could do with working on or developing, getting better at or growing into (notice the word "weakness" does not appear in this description!). It is one of the beauties (and mysteries) of life that things can always change and bend to make space for more incredible things to happen and be learned. But this does not mean that we are "broken" or need "fixing".

Focusing on the positives is such a fantastic tool to drive ourselves forward – up those ladders (and away from those snakes!). It's up to *us* whether we keep focusing on the negatives, feeling a constant pressure to change ourselves (and in some cases even writing ourselves off completely), or whether we choose to be grateful for the self-awareness of what we would like to change in order to flourish – and then give ourselves the opportunity to do this.

LETTING GO OF YOUR SELF-IMPOSED TIMELINE

One of the things that really held me back from being confident for a long time was the idea that we needed to do things in a certain way and to a certain timeline, and therefore by a certain age, in order to keep up and be deemed "successful". But life is not a race or a competition to see who can complete the most stages first. Life is precious, and can be short – so living it based on what we think we "should" be doing at each stage can make us step into, or stay in, situations that we aren't truly happy in or that make us feel like we are failing – just out of some misplaced sense of duty.

I found it really difficult to be confident in the person that I was and the choices that I made in life because I was measuring everything in my life against unrealistic, fairy-tale milestones. I was under the illusion that if my life didn't check all the boxes that I *thought* I should have achieved along the way, then I must be doing something wrong!

It's time to get a sledgehammer out and destroy the idea that certain things have to happen at certain times, or indeed that they even have to happen at all! The traditional list goes: grow up, get an education, learn to drive, establish a career, buy a property, find a spouse, get married, have children – and, ideally, do all that by the time you're 30-something! Some people may indeed do all those things by that point, but guess what: there are no rules – so set yourself free of all this unnecessary self-tyranny!

Without inducing an existential crisis, I believe that the fundamental point of life is: to live it. And living it looks different to everyone.

After school, I went to Open University for a few terms before deciding it wasn't for me. As a result, I didn't have the same university experience as many of my peers – such as living it up on campus like you see in the movies. I met Trevor and had a baby before we got married. I had no established career or high-paying job by the time I had children, as I had hoped I might. And because I hadn't done anything that I thought I was "meant" to have, when people asked me about certain aspects of my life, I generally used to either inflate the truth or try to avoid talking about it. I didn't want to admit that I hadn't "done life properly".

Not only was I measuring *myself* by this imaginary "success" timeline, I was also judging *others* who didn't fall in line with it, often projecting the insecurities I felt over my *own* circumstances on to others. I found I could only finally Own and live my best life when I let go of the stupid checklist that I had been subconsciously measuring my life against.

Accepting your life and yourself in the moment doesn't negate the fact you may want *more* for yourself in the future. But it's a key part in stepping into your own authentic confidence – and letting go of any shame or guilt about who you are and where you are in life.

BEING YOUR OWN BEST FRIEND

In order for us to be truly confident in who we are, we must live in a space where the opinion we have of ourselves is the loudest, most positive and most important.

We cannot live life surviving on the validation of others, because if you live by the praise of others, you will live by their criticism, too.

I feel most confident in the person I am now because *I like me*. I validate *myself* because my life depends on it.

Unfortunately, in today's world, we often learn to care more about what *others* think about us, and whether or not they like us, than what we think about *ourselves*. I will go into this in more depth in Chapter 4, but I want to touch on it here too, as it's such an important part of being able to just have the confidence to *be yourself*, whatever the influences of the outside world may be.

Confidence is being able to be unapologetically yourself, regardless of what others around you think or feel. In order for me to get to this point I have had to really step outside myself and be the friend that I have often needed.

There is a saying that encourages you to talk to yourself as you would to your friend, but I think it goes deeper than that. You have to love, treat and respect yourself as you would anyone else you care for and love.

I wasn't a good friend to myself for a long time. I didn't like me. I wasn't kind to me. And I was in a vicious cycle of negative self-talk and self-sabotage – feeling guilty for being horrible to myself in the first place ...

The idea of not allowing *outside* positive comments to fuel you might initially seem strange. But this is nonetheless what I suggest! In an ideal world, any positive comments from outside of yourself should only be an *added bonus* to the positive feelings that you *already* hold about yourself!

You don't need external validation to build self-confidence. It isn't the responsibility of *others* to like you – it's your *own* responsibility to ensure that you like *yourself*. Don't get me wrong, I'm not saying it doesn't feel nice when someone tells you that you've done something well or that you look great. Of course it feels fantastic! However, it becomes an issue if these are the only times you feel good about yourself, as it means that you're allowing *others* to control the feelings you hold about yourself rather than simply affirming your already existing awareness that you're a badass! Any time that your self-worth or confidence is hung onto something outside of yourself, it is a dangerous place to be – where you're likely to soon start falling down life's slippery "snakes"!

One of the best ways that I've been able to accept and embrace compliments and encouragement, but not let them become the basis for my self-worth, has been by being my own best friend. Thankfully, I do actually have a whole list of other real-life human being besties that I have collected over the years, who are truly wonderful. However, I have had to learn to be my *first* bestie and go-to in order to be able to stand firm in who I am. Then, any external positivity simply becomes a wonderful, welcome bonus to how I already feel.

Some of the most effective ways I have done this are:

Acceptance and Forgiveness Over Punishment

Can you imagine if you had done something and went to tell a friend in search of compassion and grace and, instead, they berated and punished you? Good friends simply don't behave in this way – especially not besties. Yet we are all too often willing to treat ourselves this way!

Since I have learned how to show myself that same compassion and grace – accepting and forgiving myself rather than allowing myself to wallow in frustration, anger or negativity – I have opened up more headspace, more resourcefulness and more resilience within myself, as well as more confidence.

So the next time there is something that you feel upset or even angry at yourself about, try to stop for a moment and respond to yourself as you would to a friend coming to you with the same issue.

I have been in countless conversations with friends where I have given them encouragement and advice only to find myself needing exactly the same chat later down the line. So let's make a conscious effort to be more considerate about how we respond to ourselves.

Feel free to write down some sample kind responses if you feel they might not come easy to you – you might even want to text them to yourself, voice note them or say them out loud to help get you into better habits. You deserve the same compassion and kindness that you give to others!

Comfort Over Shame

As just discussed, great friends are often the go-to people for comfort when you are in distress or feeling bad about something. They don't shame us, make us feel worse about what has happened, question why we have done it, blame us for being stupid or tell us we should have known better. Yet we often shame, rather than comfort, ourselves in our times of need, with the result of making ourselves feel even worse than we already did!

Learning to be able to comfort ourselves, especially in moments where shame would have previously presided, is key in the journey to self-love. So many times in my life I have berated myself for crying or being over-emotional, for example, yet I have often let friends cry on my shoulder for as long as they needed. These are the kinds of comforting, nurturing moments that we need to give *ourselves* permission to have – in order to feel safe with ourselves and fully trust ourselves.

There are many ways that we can offer ourselves such comfort. Some that have made a difference in my journey to more self-love and self-confidence are:

- Giving yourself permission to cry (and I mean full-on ugly cry! It feels *good*)
- Giving yourself permission to just feel how you feel; you don't always need to know what exactly is the matter
- Taking a shower or bath – to freshen up
- Hugging yourself; I know it might sound strange but throwing your arms around yourself can feel so comforting (if you find this difficult, you might want to invest in a weighted blanket instead)
- Visualizing a peaceful place where you can take a moment to breathe deeply and realign; this can be anywhere that you find calming, whether it's a meadow, a beach or a mountain
- Eating something you love, whether sushi, fruit, ice cream or a massive bar of chocolate; it's ok to give yourself permission to enjoy eating something you love
- Getting more physically comfortable, whether by changing clothes, putting on your favourite leggings or PJs, kicking off your shoes, changing your sitting position or moving around
- Watching something you love (ideally something funny); my go-to movies are *Coming to America* and *Death Becomes Her* (both absolute classics that I implore you to watch if you haven't already)

One of these ideas may work for you, a few of them might, or maybe you know *other* things that will help you when you're feeling low. Whatever your version of comfort and self-care looks like, just be sure to do it when you need to do it.

Owning It Top Tip

Make journalling a part of your daily routine that's as important as brushing your teeth. Even if you can only carve out a few minutes a day to write down your thoughts, feelings and aspirations, it will help you to get to know and trust yourself better.

Have a Laugh

Laughing at yourself can help you stop taking yourself so seriously and show yourself a bit more compassion. I recently fell over in the shower and spent the next few minutes tearing myself apart about how stupid I was to leave the shower gel out, how I could have really hurt myself and then – just to make myself feel even *more* guilty over events that hadn't even happened! – I thought about how if someone *else* had fallen and hurt themselves, it would all have been *my* fault!

When I was finally done with all the drama in my head, I went downstairs and told Trevor what had happened. Weirdly, as I started telling the story, I burst out laughing about how clumsy I had been, I realized how lucky I was not to have hurt myself, and I saw the funny side of it all! Had I reacted this way straightaway

I wouldn't have wasted my whole time in the shower being negative toward myself!

It really is worth trying to let go of things a little, loosen our often way-too-tight grip on life, and laugh at yourself more – learning to giggle at the moments you mess up rather than berating yourself for not doing them perfectly.

Not taking yourself so seriously will free up more room in your heart and mind for humour and joy. And who wouldn't want more of those in their life in place of embarrassment and shame?!

Give Yourself a Gift

Whether it is a physical gift or just allowing yourself to indulge in something you enjoy, treat yo'self! As discussed earlier, I spent many years spending money I didn't have on things that I really didn't need in order to fill a hole inside of me that felt empty – so I'm *not* suggesting that!

Instead, I'm talking about treating yourself to something lovely simply because you deserve it – a completely valid reason in and of itself! It doesn't have to be a material item (although it's totally ok if it is). It's simply about celebrating yourself!

In this spirit of self-celebration, try and do something every day – whether little or big – that is just for you. Some days, for me, this might mean having a cup of tea on my own or buying myself a magazine and letting myself sit and read uninterrupted, without feeling guilty. Other days it might mean using a luxury shower gel or having a few extra minutes in the shower in peace. Think about the things that make you smile and feel good – and show yourself the love and respect that you deserve by indulging in them.

Confidence doesn't always have to be big and bold. It can also be the quiet, internal feeling of peace and contentment that you have about yourself – the authentic feeling of knowing that you're "enough" just as you are. Whether it's about completing a task, wearing a particular outfit, dancing like you've never danced before, or making an important decision, confidence is about learning to both listen to yourself and trust yourself.

It has now been scientifically proven that people who have more self-confidence also have more self-worth and live a "happier" life. So, on this basis alone, it's worth trying every day to step further into your authentic inner confidence – because you deserve to live a life full of joy, without restrictions and without fear.

Self-Reflection Questions

On Finding & Stepping into Your Inner Confidence

- If I was to create an alter ego, who would they be, what would they be like, and why?
- Who in my life is confident and what do I value in them?
- What do I already feel confident about?
- What are my strengths? And do I find it hard to identify them?
- In what areas of my life would I like to build more confidence?
- How can I use my strengths to support growth in these areas?

GUIDED TASK
Get to Know Your "Snakes and Ladders"

We learned earlier in this chapter that the "snakes" of life are things that hold you back, drag you down and/or block your potential in life, while "ladders" are things that raise you up, encourage you and make you feel good about yourself. As well as allowing you to get to know yourself better, this task will leave you with a visual representation of both the things that drag you down in life and the things that lift you up and raise your confidence – something that you can turn to any time as a reminder of the things and people that serve you best in life (to be embraced) and the things and people that don't (to be avoided where possible!).

What To Do

1. Create two columns on a piece of paper – one with the heading "snakes" at the top, and the other with the heading "ladders". Then, under each heading, list the main things in your life that you associate with that category.

   When I first did this task, some of my "snakes" were:

   • Negative comments from my boss at work
   • Feeling like I've let my family down
   • Overthinking past circumstances

And some of my "ladders" were (and still are):

- Doing things that I love, such as journalling and being creative
- Practising regular self-care, such as scheduling in daily "me time" (even if only five minutes)
- Saying regular positive affirmations (see page 115 for a GUIDED TASK on this)

2. Once you've written down as many things in each list as come to mind, making sure you have a lot of "ladders", you might want to take the task one step further by drawing or printing your very own Snakes and Ladders board. You can then label the "snakes" and "ladders" on the board with the things that you identified in your lists.

GUIDED TASK
Identify Your Strengths

The idea of this task is to identify your strengths on paper so that you can gain more confidence in your own capabilities, and look for ways in which you can embrace them more in daily life.

What To Do

1. Look at the list of positive qualities below and see if you feel any of them are particular strengths of yours. If so, circle the three most apt. Otherwise, add your own in the spaces provided.

Honest   Loving   Friendly   Understanding

Brave   Nurturing   Loyal   Grateful

Resilient   Creative   Curious   Organized

Empathetic   Forgiving   Flexible   Fair

Kind   Good at listening   Attentive   Funny

Open-minded   Mindful   Detail-orientated   Thoughtful

Hardworking   Solution-oriented   Trustworthy   Patient

Generous   Enthusiastic   Determined   Dedicated

_____   _____

Once you have chosen your three key words, write out the following statements three times and fill in all the gaps, using each of your three chosen words to fill the blank in the first statement each time:

- I know that one of my strengths is that ...
- I already apply this in my life when ...
- I can use this strength when ...

Here's an example from when I did this task – to give you an idea of how to do it for yourself:

- I know one of my strengths is that I'm kind.
- I already apply this in my life when I'm dealing with other people.
- I can use this strength more when I'm thinking about, and talking to, myself.

2. Don't feel you have to stop at three positive qualities! Three is a good starting point, but if you feel like doing more, please do so!

The most important thing with this task is that you commit to actually putting into action the content of the last line in each of your sets of statements, as this will build your levels of both self-trust and confidence.

Chapter 3

Learning to Accept, Like & Love Yourself

What *is* love? I've asked myself this question a lot of times throughout my life, and every time I come up with a new answer: something else to add to the long list of things that love might mean. But at some point I realized that all my answers had something in common: they all focused on *other* people; never on me.

The idea of liking and loving *myself* first and foremost seemed selfish to me – and therefore uncomfortable. But the more I explored this notion, the more I came to realize that it *has* to start with me, as only *then* can I experience it fully elsewhere in my life, too! And this new perspective changed my life!

It's like when they tell you on a plane that, in case of an emergency, you need to put on your own life jacket and mask before helping others: you can't help anyone else if you don't help yourself first.

Similarly, we are only able to truly and deeply love *others* if we truly and deeply love *ourselves* first, as only then can we give from a place of overflow and abundance.

In this chapter we will mostly discuss romantic relationships, but this is only because this is where a lot of us get our ideas of what love looks and feels like. Having said that, whether you're single or in a relationship – and no matter what your romantic or sexual preferences – this chapter *will* apply to you, as love is accessible to everyone.

One thing that I *won't* be telling you is that you need a partner in order to experience love. I love my husband but I've also learned to love myself. As such, I know for sure that I could do badass love all by myself if I wasn't in a relationship.

If, however, like me, you *are* in a committed relationship, I'm by no means saying that you can't love your partner if you don't yet know how to love yourself. It's just that, in my experience, when I committed to fully accepting myself, learning to like myself and falling in love with myself, I also fell in love with my husband all over again – this time more deeply than before.

I also started to feel a deeper love for others around me, and to have a stronger sense of compassion, understanding and patience in my heart.

No longer did I feel drained or exhausted by relationships. No longer did I feel like I was giving more than I was receiving. And no longer did I find myself *craving* or *needing* the love of others to validate or heal me. Instead, I was able to just embrace their love, enjoy it and sit comfortably in it.

It hasn't been an easy ride to get here – and it's still one that I'm working on – but let me share with you how I got here, and why loving myself more than anyone else was the best decision I ever made – for everyone!

EXPECTATIONS VERSUS REALITY

I don't know if it was all the Disney movies that I watched as a child or the epic '80s and '90s R'n'B music videos, but, funnily enough, my *idea* of what love was supposed to look like wasn't quite what happened in reality. In my head, I should have been experiencing love like the besties who have each other's backs in *Thelma and Louise*, or like in every music video playing on MTV – running out into the rain to declare burning love for one another after a dramatic lovers' tiff.

I had so romanticized almost every aspect of my life in ways like this that I had unknowingly set up a completely unrealistic set of expectations! For example: I've wanted to write a book ever since I can remember, and in my mind, writing my "groundbreaking" manuscript was going to be an incredible and glamorous journey (it *is* incredible, as it happens, but glamourous it really isn't!).

I expected myself to be sitting in funky coffee shops with my laptop and a cup of exotic coffee in a terracotta mug, while I masterfully powered through a thousand very well written words every few hours. Or maybe I'd be on a sunny balcony somewhere, staring out to the ocean, with the sea air fuelling my fingers to pass over the keys as I poured my soul onto the screen.

The reality, however, is that I'm hiding from my kids in the bedroom, dressed – in what can be loosely termed "house clothes" (that's being kind!). I'm sat on a bed with no duvet cover on it, because I forgot to dry it. And there's a cold coffee sat half empty on the floor – half empty not because I drank half but because one of the kids kicked it over earlier and I haven't cleaned it up yet or got a refill. So, not quite as glamorous as I had envisaged!

Maybe I've read too many books, watched too many movies or developed too much of an obsession with the beauteous visions on Pinterest, but my idea about what a lot of my life *would* look like was *so* idealized and romanticized that it has often led to me feeling disappointed with reality, particularly when it comes to my love life!

I often look back and wonder why my friends didn't ignore my calls after a while, as the pattern of my behaviour was always the same when it came to men. I would "fall" madly in love, try to bend and twist myself into the "perfect" partner, get hurt or let down by the guy, and then stay with him anyway (in the hope that it would somehow "romantically" work out!). The guy would then finally leave me, and, heartbroken, I would cry on my friends' shoulders before finding the next guy to repeat the cycle with!

My girls must really love me because they never let me feel awful about this. Instead, they were always there to pick up the pieces of my broken heart and get me back on my feet.

As much as I love my husband, I can't say that our journey has been an easy one either, as I went into our relationship with all sorts of issues from before I met him. And one thing that's harder than trying to heal from your *past* relationships is trying to do that while you're in a *new* relationship! After all, how can you support someone else with their needs when you haven't yet identified and met many of your own?! Do I wish I had had a bit more time to myself before committing to my husband? Yes, sometimes. But I also know that I wouldn't be where I am today without having gone through the experience of having to juggle my *own* healing with all the ups and downs of being in a new relationship at the same time.

EXPLORING DADDY ISSUES

I don't want to go straight ahead and say, "Daddy issues were what landed me in some of the very messy, love-related predicaments I have been in", but Daddy issues *were* what landed me in some of the very messy, love-related predicaments I have been in!

Now some backstory: my Mum was a backing singer on tour when she got pregnant with me at 20 (sounds like a movie, right?). Nine months later, after living her best life on the road for as long as she could, there I was – a little bouncing baby. It was just me and my Mum. Until, that is, she met my brother's Dad when I was around four, and it became my Mum, my brother and me – a trio that was (and still is) a force to be reckoned with.

I have since connected with my biological Dad and his family (that story is for another time). And, hand on heart, I don't have any negative feelings toward him, them or the situation. In fact, I feel grateful that they have been able to be part of my life, even if only more recently. However, I would be lying if I said that having an absent father throughout the majority of my life had no effect on me, especially when it came to my relationships with men.

I don't have memories of any big dramas between my parents. There was no messy breakup or divorce. Nobody left anyone. In fact, I never even knew who my Dad was until I was older. My Mum never spoke badly of him, and there was nothing that ever made me think that him not being around was an issue for me, or causing any sort of traumatic childhood experience. However, after a lot of soul-searching, I realized that, for me, the fact that he knew I existed yet had decided not to be there for me always left a hole in my heart. A hole from which voices would often whisper, "He just didn't *want* you".

I don't remember at what age I started feeling this, but I know that I wasn't old enough to really understand the impact that having a baby would have on someone. In my mind, my Dad just knew I existed but didn't want to see me.

It wasn't until I became a parent myself and started to unpack feelings like this in therapy that I realized how this seed of a thought had grown and grown as I got older – planting itself in every romantic relationship that I fell into. It took me a while to really accept and understand that many of my negative patterns in relationships were a lot to do with me craving love and affection, no matter how it looked. I was just grateful to *be* in a relationship – even when they were breaking me.

CRAVING FOR LOVE

I used to be forever trying to fall in love. The second that someone I fancied caught my eye, I was fantasizing about the wedding we would have and practising my new signature with his surname.

While I know many a woman (and man) who lets their imagination run wild in this way, let me tell you: I took it to the extreme. I'm talking Helga from *Hey Arnold* extreme (if that reference means anything to you), although thankfully not Glenn Close from *Fatal Attraction* extreme! I would become obsessed with a fantasy version of love because my idea of "love" was all based on Hollywood and Disney!

While there is, in theory, nothing wrong with crazy, mad, head-over-heels, giddy love, the issue for me was that I believed at the time that love only existed if it was shared in a *relationship*. The mere concept that love started within ourselves would have been laughable to me, and would have seemed impossible given that every example of love that I "knew" was between two or more people.

I was constantly searching for my "happy ever after", trying to fill a void that had been left in my heart by the first man who was supposed to love me the most, but who hadn't! This translated into me constantly jumping from one relationship to another in the hope that I would land somewhere firm and be able to stay there – safe and loved.

Being single was never an option for me because, to me, the label of being "single" was one that represented being alone, unloved and unwanted. As a result, I was continually "on the market" and doing everything I could to make sure I wasn't single for long.

But it wasn't just the craving for deep-rooted validation that had me on every dating website going – looking for the "plenty of fish" that they claimed were out there. Society has a special way of making you feel that if you're single, there must be something wrong with you – as if love and fulfilment can only be obtained if you're in a relationship! Thankfully, this notion seems to have been changing somewhat over the years, with even Disney movies now evolving so that men no longer come in to swoop up the princess and save the day. However, there is no denying that most people still feel more comfortable when those around them are "nicely settled" in relationships.

I once talked to one of my aunts about this. She is the epitome of an independent woman, and she told me that the main reason she was single, and happily so, was that she didn't want to be reliant on someone else for love. After all, there are no guarantees in life! It doesn't matter how much someone loves you, how many promises they make or what legal documents you both sign (such as a marriage certificate), anyone can do anything at any time, leaving you vulnerable and exposed. For her, she therefore decided that the best thing she could do was love and respect *herself* first.

TRUSTING YOUR INSTINCTS

There was nothing I loved more when growing up than music videos. I mean, butterfly clips and flip phones were a close second, but music videos were the biz! One in particular (which I didn't really even understand at the time) was Whitney Houston's "It's Not Right But It's Okay" circa 1998: a story about being cheated on by her partner and taking the empowered decision to end the relationship.

Now, I was clearly too fascinated by her leather ensemble in the video to pay too much attention to the full lyrics, as I missed the crucial bit about her kicking him to the kerb: "Pack your bags up and leave/Don't you dare come running back to me …". All I heard was the "It's not right but it's okay" message! And, unfortunately, my reaction to being cheated on was always in line with this: let's stay together and keep trying! Not quite the sentiment she was going for in the song. Soz Whitney! (I hope that nowadays record producers would have changed the song title to a more empowering "It's Not Right, It's Not Okay" – in line with the Me Too movement.)

The thing is, when someone cheats on you, the most hurtful part of the situation isn't necessarily the anger or frustration at the lies and the fact that you didn't trust your gut. For me, it was the fact that I was left wondering, "What's *wrong* with me? Why can *nobody* love me?"

The first experience I had of being cheated on was in a relationship that I'd always seen as me "punching above my weight" (I look back now and realize that this *really* wasn't the case! The guy wasn't all that!). I instinctively knew that something wasn't right, as I couldn't shake the feeling that I wasn't being told the truth. But I pushed those thoughts aside as they were hindering the progress of my master plan to "live happily ever after" with him.

The problem with ignoring your instincts is that the reality of things will catch up with you eventually – only to sucker punch you in your innocent little face so that you can finally see what's going on right before your eyes.

The woman that I suspected he was having an affair with decided to befriend me. She corroborated the story that he told me: that it was all in my head and I was just being paranoid. And, between them, they convinced me that I should calm down and not be so irrational. As a result, I felt I had no choice but to blame my constant bubble of anxiety about our relationship or my imagination simply getting carried away with itself!

Cutting a long, complex story somewhat short, when the truth of their affair eventually came to light, the first feeling I had wasn't anger or hurt; it was relief. Relief because I realized that I wasn't going crazy after all! I had known all along, and rather than trust myself, step away or leave them to it, I had stayed.

I hadn't stayed because he had promised to change. I hadn't stayed because we had too much to lose to let it all go. I hadn't stayed because we were going to seek professional guidance and make it work. And I hadn't stayed because we cared deeply about one another and wanted to ignite change in our lives.

I had stayed because I was simply too scared to leave and be on my own. Somewhere deep down I believed that being in a relationship with someone who was cheating on me was better than being in no relationship at all – and *this* was the issue.

I was so consumed by trying to feel love from someone who very clearly didn't love me that I didn't even consider that learning to really like and love *myself* could be the answer!

LEARNING TO FORGIVE

I have friends who have gone through betrayals but who have then sought professional support to make things better, as they wanted to rediscover the love and respect that had once been the cornerstones of their relationship. And I hugely respect this, as their decision wasn't just about their love for one *another* but also the love they each had for *themselves* – love that made them truly sorry for their transgressions and made them want the best for themselves, as well as each other.

When I finally ended the relationship that I mentioned above, however, I realized that at no point had my ex ever said sorry for the way he treated me! I'm a firm believer that sorry is just a word, and that if someone really wants to apologize, they will take action to *show* you how regretful they are and how much they love you. But in this particular scenario, my partner never even uttered the word sorry in its most basic form! And, unfortunately, I ended up carrying the pain of this into every subsequent romantic relationship that I entered into.

Forgiveness is something that can often only feel possible when someone shows remorse and makes an active change in their behaviour. So what do you do when someone doesn't do this, whether in a romantic relationship or otherwise? Maybe they just *aren't* sorry? Maybe they don't want to admit it? Maybe they can't face the truth of their own behaviour?

In some ways, it shouldn't really matter to you *why* they can't bring themselves to apologize for what they have done and how they have hurt you. This is because forgiveness is never really *for* or *about* the other person; it is for, and about, *you*. It is not about "allowing", justifying or in any way condoning what has happened. Rather, it is about your own personal healing journey – taking the first brave and humble steps toward being able to move on from the hurt that you have lived through, without negatively projecting it into other areas of your life.

For me, as crazy as it might initially sound, forgiving my ex – and also the "friend" who had betrayed me – turned out to be a life-changing act of extreme self-love. It was about me *Owning* the hurt that they had caused and accepting that I couldn't change it, but also recognizing that it didn't have to define me. It was about me taking my own power back and allowing myself to write my *own* story from here on out.

I won't get into the nitty gritty of the story now (maybe in the next book!), but the whole thing was something that I found incredibly hard to accept and understand, and it left me feeling broken, bitter, frustrated and resentful.

After several years of no contact with them and me trying my best to move on with my life, I realized at some point just how much I was still holding on to negative feelings toward them. It made it worse that each of them seemed to be living their best lives, without an apparent care in the world about the devastation they had caused me.

However, one day when I was feeling really down about not being able to move on happily, it struck me to ask myself what the benefit was of me holding on to all this anger and pain? Given that the other parties were moving on with their lives, the only person who was truly suffering was me! And I didn't deserve that! To this day, I am unsure why but, rather than feeling sorry for myself, cursing their names and wishing that bad things would happen to them (as I had done many times before!), I instead decided to pray for them! Now, whether you're religious or not, and whether you pray or not, this isn't about the way in which I processed this; it's about the effect that a simple act of loving forgiveness went on to have my life.

I prayed that they were safe and happy, that they didn't come to any harm and that they wouldn't ever go through the kind of pain that they had put me through. I prayed that they could come to terms in their own way with the trust that they had broken with me and that they could learn from what they had done so that they wouldn't do it to anyone else in the future. I forgave them for everything that had happened. And, although it felt weird at the start, once I got going, I couldn't stop! It was as if I just couldn't *bear* to live any longer with so much hate, resentment and bitterness weighing my heart down.

And I felt so freeeeee afterwards – as if an enormous weight had been lifted from my shoulders! While I still acknowledged the pain and subsequent devastation of what had happened to me, I had well and truly let go of the hot iron that had been burning me for all this time – and I started to heal. But forgiving *others* is only ever *part* of the equation; the person I needed to forgive the most was little old *me*!

FORGIVING YOURSELF

I came to realize as I travelled on my journey of self-healing that I was carrying a lot of blame and shame with me from the hurtful experiences in my life – particularly my experiences in romantic relationships.

On thinking about this, I realized that I would often tell myself that it was "my fault" that someone betrayed me in whatever way. If only I had done more, been sexier, been less argumentative, been kinder, nicer, prettier, slimmer, or whatever else. If only I had not been so *me*, then maybe they wouldn't have done what they did! I carried the burden of whatever happened on my shoulders and directed a lot of the anger, frustration and pain inward. And it weighed me down.

Taking my first steps on the path to self-forgiveness has therefore been a complete game changer for me, opening up the space for me to authentically like and love myself again.

STEPS TO SELF-FORGIVENESS

In this section, I share with you some of the key things that have helped me on my journey to self-forgiveness – in the hope that they will help you, too. It's a process that can be painful, frustrating and confusing at times. But it's so worth all the tears in the end!

Accept Where You Are

No matter how much we might like to press rewind at times in order to go back in time and do certain things differently, we can't change what has happened in the past. As such, it's essential that we embrace where we have got to in life based on the decisions that we have made. And while the route we took to get here may not always have been ideal, we're lucky enough to be here, now. This doesn't have to be our final destination though – so what matters is that, as well as *accepting* where we are, we also purposefully decide how we would like to move forward from here.

Let Go of Guilt and Shame

Guilt and shame: these two characters have stayed as close to me throughout my life as a toddler does when you're eating something tasty. They have been around forever and, while I could do with both of them making a sharp exit, guilt can, at least, help you to learn from mistakes you make. Shame, on the other hand, just makes you want to run away and hide forever – and that doesn't get anyone anywhere. Neither of them are helpful when you're trying to move forward with your life though – so it's time to give yourself a break by gently letting go of them and instead leaning into the fact that you've always done the best you could, with the best of intentions.

Lead with Compassion

Leading with compassion is hard, and, at times, can feel damn near impossible – especially when someone has done something that has hurt you deeply. But choosing to forgive – both yourself and others – is already an act of living more compassionately.

Aiming to put yourself in the position of others so that you can try to see things from their point of view is extremely useful, as it allows you to detach yourself from situations a little and see that things are often less personal to you than you might have imagined – often coming from worries or insecurities in the lives of the other parties involved.

Be Patient

The journey to forgiveness comes with its own unique set of triggers – things that are likely to remind you of past pains and that can, if you're not careful, take you straight back into feeling angry, resentful and potentially even wanting revenge. So, it's essential to be patient with yourself and give yourself plenty of time to deal with both the ups and downs that you'll inevitably go through as you try to put the art of forgiveness more and more into practice.

I'm probably one of the most impatient people I know. I want results straightaway. And I want to see evidence that what I'm doing is making a difference. But this just isn't always possible as you unlearn a lifetime worth of self-negligence, self-doubt and maybe even self-loathing.

So, as you set out on this winding and bumpy road of forgiveness, show yourself the patience and kindness that you would show someone learning any *other* new skill.

TWO HALVES DON'T MAKE A WHOLE

Most romantic relationships are made up of two individuals. But, despite what those necklaces that fit together into one heart might suggest, the two individuals in a couple are *not* two halves coming together to make a whole. I don't believe in someone being the yin to your yang or the moon to your stars. To me, you are both whole people and you come together to share that wholeness with the other person – not to provide them with something that they are lacking, but to mutually share love and joy.

My constant need to be validated by my relationship status meant that my reliance on any partners was almost always too much. As such, there was immense pressure for my partner to be *everything* I needed – and that's an impossible task for *anyone* to live up to! No matter how much they may try, they will never be able to fill that hole within the other person.

Below are some signs that you may be relying too much on your partner for your happiness and that you need to do more work to seek it from within yourself:

- A constant need for reassurance
- Seeking your partner's opinions not because they add value, but for basic validation
- Equating happiness or stability with just being in a relationship, regardless of whether or not you are in a good place within that relationship
- Being uncomfortable when your partner goes anywhere without you
- Being untrusting when they've given you no reason to distrust
- *Your* mood depending on theirs, for example, if they're unhappy when you're happy, it's likely to bring *you down* rather than you bringing *them up*

When I realized that I had been displaying most of these signs – in most (if not all!) of my past relationships, it highlighted to me just how much I needed to start giving *myself* all the nice things that I was craving from my partner. Understanding this and starting to put in the work to make it happen was like someone releasing the pressure valve on my expectations from everyone else in my life!

And this wasn't just in my romantic relationships. It was also in a lot of friendships and family dynamics. I've therefore had to actively look inward for a lot more self-validation over the years – so that all the love and reassurance I'm lucky enough to get from my husband, friends and family can just be *added bonuses* to how I already feel about myself.

LEAD BY EXAMPLE

In order to have healthy, thriving relationships that are filled with love, we need to lead by example with the way we show love to *ourselves*. Let me elaborate. Someone once said to me, "Your children will do as you *do*; not as you say". This not only led to some massive behaviour changes on my part when I was around them, but also gave me a lot to think about regarding how I behave toward *myself*. I learned that people will show love for me in the way that I love *myself*, not in the way that I ask them to.

We therefore have to love and respect ourselves so much that it shows outwardly. This way, we automatically teach others how we want to be treated, and the high standard that we expect!

SELF-LOVE IN ACTION

Learning to love yourself is a continuous process with no final destination – a beautiful journey of discovery and learning. Here follows a range of the regular practices that I do to support the growth of my self-love. These practices have been key for me to see that I am fully capable of providing *myself* with the security, stability and joy that I once thought could only come to me from *other* people.

Celebrate Yourself

Whether it's your birthday, you have achieved something special or you're just having a particularly good day(!), it's good to be able to celebrate yourself when you feel like it, and, in so doing, let others know how important marking your successes in some way is to you.

Many a time, I've made the mistake of lying low regarding my achievements because I felt it was best to be perceived as humble, "no fuss", low maintenance and easily pleased. In reality, however, more often than not I wanted to feel like a queen! Who doesn't at times? I was trying to be something that I thought *others* wanted from me, rather than embracing my true self and just asking for a fuss to be made! These days, I'm honest about it and lead by example, so if I want a fuss making, then I'll be the first one to make it!

Articulate Your Needs

Who doesn't love a surprise, eh? But not everyone will know what we want unless we are open and honest enough to simply tell them! It took me a long time to realize that it's often easier to just *tell* my husband some of the things that I want, rather than getting angry if he doesn't meet the expectations that he had zero clue about in the first place!

If we want our relationships to be happy and fulfilling, it's important to be clear about *all* aspects of our wants and needs, and to be able to have frank conversations with our loved ones about them.

This goes for friends and family as well as partners. People can't always know when we need something from them. And this means they may not call you at the right moment or give you quite the right gift. But this doesn't mean that they don't care!

We have to love ourselves enough to let them *know* what we need from them so that they have an opportunity to give it to us – before we consume ourselves with anxiety about whether or not they really love us!

Be the Person You Need

We have touched on this topic already but, because it's such a key aspect of truly loving yourself, let's refresh our memory, eh? It's so very important to be the person, and the friend, that you need for yourself – someone you can rely on in both good times and bad.

When I stopped expecting loved ones to provide me with the things that I didn't think I could do for myself and, instead started doing them for *myself*, it gave me a whole new level of love and appreciation for myself. And an added bonus was that anything my friends and family then did for me felt like this beautiful, enriching overflow for which I was extraordinarily grateful.

Don't Believe Everything You Think

Consider for a moment all the times when you have told yourself that you are fat, ugly, useless, unworthy of receiving love, or any other such negative crap! Then take a moment to let it sink in that just because these things have been said (whether by yourself or anyone else), it doesn't make them true! They are just thoughts and/or statements. *Not* truths. So there is no need to take them on board and believe them. They do not serve you.

Fall in Love with Yourself

Take some time out and ask yourself the kind of questions that you would ask someone you had just started dating. What are your hobbies? What values do you try to live by? What do you want from life? And so on … This will allow you to get to know yourself better, develop a better relationship with yourself, and see just how incredible and loveable you truly are.

Create Pockets of Peace

I'm obsessed with this wonderful blogger on TikTok called Nabela, who started a series called "Pockets of Peace". In it, she encourages you to find just a few moments each day to create a sense of peace for yourself. You can decide to just breathe, to practise gratitude, or to do anything else (whether big or small) that will show yourself how important you are. I've been adopting this daily practice for a while now and it's made a big difference to how I feel life about myself.

Embrace *All* of You

It's important to fully embrace *everything* about yourself – your incredible heart and soul as well your incredible body (see Chapter 5 for more on this) and incredible mind. This might encompass all kinds of things – from the kindness you show others, the joy you bring to any occasion, the great listener you are, and whatever else. Remind yourself of these things daily and be proud of them in the knowledge that they are just small parts of what make you the wonderful person that you are.

Expect Change

Like most things in life, our self-love needs are forever evolving. How I needed to show myself love at the start of my healing journey and how I need to do so at *this* point in my life is different. Each stage is valid, so allow space for these changes. Know that you are not getting anything wrong. Just follow your instincts, and know that truly loving yourself isn't always going to look the same – and that's ok.

Don't Compare Your Self-Love

Showing love for yourself through self-care practices isn't a "one size fits all" thing. It will look and feel different for all of us. The fundamental part is that we should all do it!

I thought for a long time that self-care had to be all about bath bombs and drinking green juice – and it is for some people. But green juices aren't for me (although I am totally down for the bath bombs!). The trick is to define what *your* love looks like for *you*. Is it setting boundaries with those around you? Taking your lunch break at work every day? Indulging in a nurturing daily skincare routine? Whatever it may look like for you, there's no need to compare it to what anyone else is doing, as it's impossible to be doing it wrong! You are doing it for you – and you alone!

Find Your Happy Place

Where and with whom can you just be you? When do you feel the most loved and joyful? What are you doing, wearing, eating or drinking during these moments? Once you know, then do more of the same! Doing *more* of the things that make us feel good allows us to know what that is like and really recognize it, so that we can do it again and again ... and again.

Show Love, Even When it's Hard

This sounds a bit odd, but I've learned that showing love and compassion even to those who have maybe not shown it to us will raise our level of love for ourselves, allowing us to stay in a more positive and loving mindset. I'm not encouraging anyone to stay in relationships that are negative, of course, but even when we walk away from these, it can be done in a spirit of kindness. Not everyone will repay this love and kindness to you but that's not your issue; it's theirs.

Be Realistic

I don't know anyone in the world who is happy and loving 24 hours a day, 7 days a week. I know that I certainly have moments where I don't feel like that at all – where I want to just stay in bed and hide. And while that is kind of impossible with three kids, I do it when I can. I let myself have a day here and there where I eat *all the food*, watch all the movies that make me cry, and wallow in my own feelings. Allowing myself this time is an act of self-love, as it reminds me that I don't always have to have it all together. It also reminds me that we're all just human and that it's fine – and "real" – to have down days now and again, or days where it's all a bit much!

Let it Go

Like Elsa (if you know, you know), just let it go! I've had to learn to let go of a lot of past hurts in order to step into authentic love. Doing this often requires professional support. I still go to therapy, and it is one of the best things I have done and continue to do.

I no longer live in my past, holding on to moments that weigh me down and make my journey to self-love so much more difficult. Any journey where you're carrying a heavy load is going to be harder, slower and more difficult. Thankfully, I've learned to leave behind the luggage containing all the things that are no longer supporting me – in order to move forward with more lightness and ease.

Owning It Top Tip

Stop playing the comparison game! I challenge you to not compare yourself to anyone else for a whole day – in the hope that if you embrace yourself in your own right for long enough and often enough (without worrying about others), this healthy attitude might stick for good!

SELF-LOVE VERSUS SELF-CARE

Self-care, to me, is the physical action of caring for yourself. It's the bath bombs, the spa days, the mindfulness sessions and the "treat yo'self" moments. Self-love, on the other hand, is the unconditional, unwavering feeling that lets you know that you *deserve* self-care and gives you permission to show yourself this kindness.

Self-care looks different for everyone. So, in order to define what it looks like for *you*, firstly have a think about what you love, what feels good for you and what you need. Then do things that support these needs as often as you can. It's important to be consistent and proactive with this, even when you're feeling gooood. That way, your self-care rituals will be easier to keep up on bad days, when you most need them.

Some of my favourite ways to practise self-care – in order to boost my sense of love for myself – are to:

Get Outside

It is a known fact that being in nature can help you feel better. I've heard a lot of talk about how particularly good it is for you to step out barefoot, as it can help you feel more grounded and connected. Weird fact about me though: I hate walking on grass barefoot! There's something about the texture that makes me feel all weird inside (as well as the prospect of potential spiders, of course). But thankfully I enjoy getting outside when I keep my shoes on! Whether you go for a local walk, head to the coast, walk on the grass or even just open all the windows in your home to let in some fresh air, reconnecting on some level with nature can make a big difference.

Move that Body

Walk, run, dance, hula hoop, wiggle your toes ... It doesn't matter how moving your body looks for you; it's just important that you do it! I'm not the biggest fan of "official exercise", but I'm a huge fan of a kitchen disco party, so that's how I most often move my body, and it feels great. How do you move yours?

Indulge in a Skincare Routine

I'm not talking a 200-step skincare routine with products that are sourced from an exclusive cave in the middle of nowhere and cost $675 for a tiny tube! I'm just talking about giving yourself a few minutes in the morning where you dedicate the time to looking after yourself by indulging in a bit of facial cream, serum, SPF, etc!

Read & Learn

Giving myself the chance to expand my knowledge – in order to become a better person for both myself and others – has been brilliant for me. Whether I'm reading a self-help book or watching an episode of *Blue Planet*, I adore having my eyes opened to new

things, people, places, cultures and all the rest. What better gift
to yourself than to widen your horizons in this way.

YOU CAN'T GET THIS WRONG

It may feel like there's a lot to do on your journey to self-love, and,
in a way, there is (sorry!). But please don't let that put you off, as
you cannot get this wrong. My hope is that this chapter will act as a
springboard of ideas for you – encouraging you to try at least a little
bit at a time. You have nothing to lose and everything to gain ...

Self-Reflection Questions

On Learning to Accept, Like & Love Yourself

- What and who in life makes me feel the most loved?
- What things do I love most about myself?
- What self-care practices can I introduce to my life that
  will boost my sense of self-love?
- Am I holding on to any negative emotions or beliefs
  from past hurtful events?
- How can I learn and grow, with love, from past
  negative experiences?
- Are there people in my life who it would be useful for
  me to forgive?

GUIDED TASK
Affirmation Writing

Affirmations are positive statements that we can say to ourselves to encourage us on our journey to self-love. Saying them regularly supports an empowered mindset by creating *positive* self-talk that challenges any underlying *negative* thoughts and beliefs.

Do They Really Work?

Daily affirmations have been a big part of my personal journey, helping me to become more optimistic and confident by constantly reminding me that there's good to see in everything. The key to them having an impact is to use them as regularly and consistently as possible.

What To Say

It's completely up to you what you want your affirmations to, well, "affirm" in your life. One of the most important things I realized when writing affirmations for myself was that I didn't need to overthink them. When I started, I focused too much on trying to make them "perfect", rather than just tuning into what I most needed to hear at the time. I have since created a mini formula to make it easier for myself. This involves me using three statements every day to help guide my affirmations:

- I choose ...
- I will ...
- I am ...

Regular affirmations of mine include:

- I choose to be happy
- I will overcome my struggles
- I am a great mother and friend

Now write some affirmations for *yourself* using this 3-step method.

What do you need to hear from yourself right now?

Chapter 4

Dealing with "Mean Girls" & Naysayers

Not many things are guaranteed in this world. Unfortunately, one of the few things that's a given is that not everyone in life is going to like you or be nice to you. For a self-diagnosed people-pleaser like myself, this has been one seriously hard pill to swallow – and one that, if I'm honest, I'm still chewing on, on a pretty much daily basis.

Given the vast number of people in the world, it's kind of inevitable that you won't be everyone's "cup of tea", and we would be kidding ourselves if we didn't admit there were a fair few people that we're probably not too keen on ourselves.

I once read a quote that said: "Stop trying to be liked by everybody; *you* don't even like everybody" – and it made me giggle because it's so true! However, it's one thing knowing, in theory, that you can't please all of the people all of the time, and another thing really learning to truly accept this and figure out how to deal with it. I mean, what do you *do* when people bring all kinds of negativity to your door?

We all experience "mean girls" (and boys!) and naysayers at different times in our lives – and in different ways. And our reactions to them will depend on lots of things, including where, who and how the negativity is presented to us.

The thing is that negativity doesn't always show up as someone being *obviously* rude and hurtful to us. It can also show its ugly head in the form of passive aggressive comments, patronizing remarks, backhanded compliments, and all sorts of other things.

When I reflect on a lot of my interactions with people in the past that felt a little "off" but which I just brushed off as me being paranoid, I now realize that I had every reason to feel uncomfortable about many of them as they simply weren't "nice"!

Can you think of any moments like that in *your* life? Maybe a colleague who has said something that made you feel insulted but that you, or others, have brushed off as you being overly sensitive or just "taking it the wrong way"? Or maybe a friend who subtly undermines you any time you're sharing how you're feeling, but who you let get away with it as they're generally good to you otherwise. I don't want you to overthink every communication you've ever had, wondering if it was ok. But I *do* want to just really highlight the fact that negativity isn't always as obvious as you might expect!

I've experienced it personally on so many different levels – both online and in "real life". And, while I've learned over time that different people and different situations require different reactions, I've also learned that we simply cannot control what others think or do; all that we can control is how we allow it to affect our *own* lives.

BEING AWARE OF OLD WOUNDS

While a lot of my experience of negative comments and "bullying" has been online (through The Fat Funny One social media), this isn't the only area of my life where judgements, assumptions and horrible comments have had a profound effect on how I felt about myself and how I was perceived by those around me. Whether hurtful or offensive comments come from family, friends, colleagues, random people on the street or anyone else, they can really shake the very foundations that you believe you were built on.

I've had all sorts of comments directed at me about who people believe I am – sometimes with regards to my size, sometimes the colour of my skin, sometimes my parenting style and my children; how often (or how little) I work; how I make money and how I spend that money; and genuinely almost anything that makes me who I am.

For a long time, I just couldn't shake the comments. They would dictate how I would behave and what I would share online. But, most worryingly, they would dictate how I felt about *myself*, as the comments would often affirm deep-rooted insecurities that I was trying hard to weed out. Despite this, I stayed online. I stayed because I didn't want to let anyone else win, and I knew there was more that I wanted to share with this incredible growing community.

I can honestly tell you that I've had some of the most horrific things said to me in a very loud and open manner – things that I would never dream of saying to another person. Yet they haven't always been said to me by someone else – not by an online troll, not by a bully at school or work, not by friends or family behind my back; they have been said to me by myself! So why does it feel so much worse (like a horrible sucker punch) when someone *else* says something bad to you? After all, you've been speaking badly to yourself for years!

But let's think about this: have you ever had a paper cut? (Honestly, how can something so small be so painful!?) Or, if not a paper cut, maybe you've experienced something small but sore like a graze? Nothing that requires a massive bandage or a trip to the doctor, but something that really hurts for a while, and that you can then almost forget about as the pain fades. I mean, you know, it's still there, but you can live with it and get on with things. However, then, one day, you decide to slice a lemon and boom! – your hand feels like it's about to fall off, and the pain is unbearable!

Considering I've had three children, I imagine that talking about a paper cut like this seems somewhat dramatic, but I'm sure you get what I mean! When someone comes at you with a nasty or negative comment, an insult or just a remark that makes you feel "less than", it can feel like they're pouring lemon juice all over your still sensitive paper cut! It stings and it burns. But the important thing to bear in mind is that the original injury wasn't caused by this other person; they have just played a part in making your old wound hurt more.

Now, I'm not saying that we deliberately choose to give ourselves paper cuts! But such wounds do tend to happen over the years. And, whether we are 12, 24, 44 or 64, it can still hurt when someone pours lemon juice on them, or rubs salt in them! However, the good news is that it doesn't matter how long they have been there! We are able to heal them with the love we can learn to give to ourselves …

HAVING THE COURAGE TO BE DISLIKED

While being bullied (something that we'll discuss later in this chapter) is often one of the most recognized ways of being treated badly, it isn't something that everyone has experienced. However, just because you haven't been a victim of *direct* bullying doesn't mean that you haven't experienced negative treatment at the hands of others.

The reality is that not everyone will be kind all of the time, even if *you* are the most kind, loving and generous person in the world. You can be as beautiful and wonderful as a ray of sunshine, and there will, unfortunately, still be people who treat you badly or don't like you – simply because they prefer the heat to the rain, or maybe because, at the core of things, they don't like *themselves* and don't know what to do with all that loathing and frustration.

It isn't easy to get comfortable with anyone telling you that there's something they dislike about you. But, luckily, this isn't your burden to carry – it's the other person's. I completely get that there are probably some people in your life who you feel obligated to listen to and/or to please. But for every reason that you may feel there is to go along with these people's views, there are countless more as to why you shouldn't! The essential is to be brave enough to just *be yourself* – irrespective of what anyone else might think, say or do!

STAYING AWAY FROM THE FIRE

If you were told that there was danger of a fire ahead, would you keep moving forward and lean into it, or stay away and take a different route – in order to keep your distance?

People's negative opinions could be viewed as such a fire – from which it would be smart to keep your distance for your own safety! There's no point moving toward it when there would be no benefit for you. After all, even if you just wanted to listen to the comments of the naysayers a little bit (to get a feel for what was being said about you), there's a chance that by moving closer to the flames you'd get burned!

I had a situation once at work when I heard three of my colleagues talking unpleasantly about me in the staff kitchen. I had got up to go and make a drink and be friendly (always the one wanting to make friends), but as I had approached the kitchen door, I heard my name being mentioned, so I slowed down and leaned in to listen. "What is she even *wearing* today? She looks awful!", "Oh gosh, I know, where does she even shop?" The conversation got nastier from here on in, but rather than walk away to a safe distance, where I couldn't feel the burn of their words, I leaned in. I listened for what felt like hours, but was probably only a few brief moments, of them tearing me apart. The things they said left me well and truly burned, and I lived with the emotional scars from that for long after it happened. For years after the event, I thought about different ways that I could have handled the situation for a better outcome.

I wondered about if I had just walked in confidently and started making a cup of tea, what would they have done? If I had gone in and just asked them why *they* were all wearing what they were, would they have answered me? I thought time and time again of all the ways that I could have stood up for myself and stopped them being so horrible about me. But the reality is that the only control I had at the time was over myself. I could only have prevented myself from feeling the extended pain of it if I had simply walked away. Instead, I had made a choice to lean in and allow myself to get more burned.

So learn from my mistake, if you will: protect your heart at all costs and, if there does seem to be danger of "fire" ahead of you, keep your distance.

AVOIDING OTHERS' IDEAL VERSION OF YOU

Throughout our lives, we are surrounded by so many people – friends, family, colleagues, friends of friends, loose acquaintances; the list goes on! Those who are fortunate enough to be close to us, or to have known us for a long time, often build up a picture in their minds of how they think our lives should look, based on *their* perception of what it is like to be us. In this section, I want to consider the impact that such opinions of others can have on who we think we are and what we choose to do with our lives.

Don't get me wrong – I know that, deep down, most of our loved ones usually want the *best* for us – and to see us happy. The problem is that their notion of what "the best" looks like for us doesn't always match *our* notion of this, because no matter how much they *try* to see things from *our* point of view, they can only ever see our life through *their* eyes.

If you try and become a version of yourself that *other* people want, you will never be the true you. Being *you* is your superpower! So if you change yourself to please others (whether knowingly or not), you give *away* this power. You can really only Own your life when you get entirely comfortable with being *authentically you* all of the time (even if this doesn't match the ideal version that *others* seem to want).

It isn't easy to get to this stage. You will often have to stand strong against other people's beliefs, confident that the best version of you is when *you* are the happiest; not when they think you *should* be happy!

Another downside to being willing to bend your life to match someone else's "ideal view" of you is that you're likely to be setting yourself up to fail! This is because trying to become someone that isn't naturally you, and that has been dreamt up by someone else, means you will always be measuring yourself by standards that *they* have set. You're therefore likely to get caught in a vicious cycle of feeling like you're letting them down and then trying to change even more to become the person they want you to be! As a result, you move further and further away from your true self, and, as with any journey, the further away you go, the longer the journey back. So, for example, if your parents have high hopes for you to take on a particular career path that you don't *hate* but that isn't what you feel truly passionate about, you will likely continue to feel as if you're letting them down even if you *do* follow that path, because your decision will not have been with your whole heart. Your parents' expectations of you will therefore continue to feel like a goal that you can't ever reach. Whereas, in reality, it's your *own* goals that you should be reaching for; not theirs!

STOP GIVING PERMISSION

Nobody can make you feel anything without your consent. I spent a long time sitting with this before I truly accepted just how much is in my control.

In the past, when I had a disagreement with someone – whether a friend, colleague, family member or even my husband – I often found myself thinking about how the interaction had "*made* me feel". I would be adamant that the person in question had *made* me feel whatever it was that I was experiencing, and that the negative feelings I now had toward myself were a direct result of *their* actions.

Now, don't get me wrong, there are consequences for the actions people take. However, the fact remains that nobody can *make* us feel anything that we don't choose to feel. Have you ever tried to reason with a child? That is all the evidence you need that you cannot *make* anyone feel anything without their consent.

An exercise, recommended by my therapist, that really helped me to grasp this and put it into action was to imagine, when anyone said anything negative about me, that they were handing me a permission slip that I had to sign if I was willing to give my consent to feeling whatever it was they were offering. For example, if a colleague at work said something disparaging to me, I would imagine that they were handing me a slip of paper that said "You will feel inferior", and that I had the choice whether or not I accepted and signed off on this. Simply knowing that it was *my* choice empowered me to say no when I felt the need: "No, I'm not willing to feel inferior by taking what you want to 'dump' on me. Here's your slip back. No consent given."

I've said it before, and I will no doubt say it many more times, as it's so damn crucial: you are not responsible for what other people do or say to you; you are only in control of how, when or even *if* you allow it to affect *you* and *your* well-being.

I was once labelled as "bossy" by a colleague at work. At first, I thought that there was a bit of a compliment in there (or surely they wouldn't have said it to me!). But when I enquired further and they started to do impressions of how they viewed me at work, I soon realized that they didn't mean it in any way positively! By labelling me as "bossy" they were tagging me as aggressive, inconsiderate of other's feelings and wanting to dictate to others, which simply wasn't true. Nonetheless, I carried the weight of this label around with me for years, often using a lot of energy trying to suppress what I believed to be this negative side of me, because I was convinced that if *they* thought this about me, then so must everyone else.

Years later, I found out that the person calling me "bossy" had actually been threatened by my assertiveness; and this sense of threat had led them to *perceive* me as being bossy. So the whole thing actually had very little to do with me at all! Yet I had to recognize that it was me who had chosen to carry the burden of the label when I could have simply rejected it as something that didn't serve me in any way.

OTHERS DON'T KNOW BEST

It can be all too easy when you're not feeling confident in yourself to feel like everyone else knows better than you. But the truth is that nobody will ever be more invested in your life than you are! *You* live the consequences of the decisions you make and the actions you take each day. It's therefore *you* who has to be in the driver's seat, comfortable with the direction that you are moving in (even if you have moments of doubt now and then about whether you are going the right way).

This can be a difficult thing to put into practice, especially if you're hearing the opinions of people really close to you, such as parents or guardians. Yet I know that, even as my children's mother, I will not always know what's best for them. I may be able to do my best in guiding, supporting and making decisions that I *feel* would be best for them (especially while they are young), but, ultimately, *they* will know what's best for them, what will bring them most joy and what will bring them most peace.

There is often a hierarchy of people within our lives, and the "higher" people are within this, the more influence they have on us. For many, parents and grandparents are at the top, then siblings, partners, friends and colleagues. The list will be different for different people, but this is the standard for the majority. Given the increased level of impact from those at the "top", it's often harder to deal with interactions that are negative from the people there. But that's not to say it's impossible!

No matter how well anyone knows you, you will always know, deep down, what the right thing for yourself is; it's just a matter of trusting yourself. It's therefore important to give yourself the space to think before making any decisions based on the advice or guidance of others.

The more conscious decisions that we make for ourselves, where we are fully accountable for the outcome and can learn from the choices that we make, the more we will learn what's best for us.

SETTING BOUNDARIES

You cannot change the *people* around you, but you can change the people *around* you. No, that's not a typo! Read it again. It took me a few times to get my head around it but when I did, my Mind. Was. Blown.

The people around you may not be able to have their opinions, feelings, values or ideals changed, but you have a choice just how close *around* you they remain. And you can establish this by setting boundaries!

Boundaries are basic guidelines that you can set in your life in order to put in place what you will and won't accept in terms of the behaviour of others toward you. Contrary to what some people think, they are *not* blockers or rules that stop relationships from thriving. In fact, when implemented effectively, they can do the complete opposite, encouraging healthy, respectful relationships – whether romantic, professional or personal.

In the past, boundaries were only something that I tended to think about in terms of romantic relationships, and, even then, I was awful at upholding any. But once I started asserting some in my life, I realized just how valuable they are, and also just how much I had been putting others before myself for most of my life – whether it was their feelings, mental well-being, physical health or whatever else. I had constantly been making decisions that had positive impacts on the people *around* me but negative impacts on *me*, because I was just too afraid to ruffle anyone's feathers!

Some of the boundaries that I have set since then have completely changed my life. I now have more freedom, feel more empowered, enjoy closer and healthier relationships with loved ones, and I am finally putting myself first (which doesn't make me selfish by the way; it actually makes me a better friend, partner, daughter and mother, which is what I'm constantly aiming to be!).

As such, setting boundaries is an important act of self-care. It's a way of protecting yourself and your space, which you are well within your rights to do. It can feel like an awkward thing to do at first – and may even feel rude – as we are so heavily conditioned to always be kind and courteous to others and not to cause any "issues". But it is absolutely ok to put boundaries in place, and to review and change them whenever you feel you need to.

The three most powerful and life-changing boundaries that I have implemented in my life (and that I cannot recommend highly enough) are:

- Just say no!
- Make time for yourself
- Say "I don't want to talk about this"

So let's look at each of these in a little more depth.

Just Say No!

We all need to start saying no with the confidence and authority that a toddler has when you ask them to give you something that they shouldn't be holding.

Historically though, I've always been a "yes" person. Even when I've *wanted* to say no, I've often said yes. And when I've *really* wanted to say no, I've often said "maybe"!

On becoming more aware of this over the years, I've realized that it's because I've always hated the idea of offending people or letting them down in any way, even if doing what they suggest would be a pressure on me or impact on my wellbeing – whether physical, emotional, financial or otherwise.

My first experience of setting boundaries by saying no was declining a friend who wanted to come over for a cup of tea. I know this doesn't seem like a big deal! But I found saying no so difficult that I would often make things unnecessarily complicated when it came to doing it! I might start with ignoring a message or making up an excuse, and end up telling a white lie that I was busy or unavailable, when I was blatantly just sat at home in my underwear, watching Netflix! But, on this occasion, I decided I was just going to be honest and tell my friend that, as much as I love her, I just didn't feel like seeing anyone today and I would like to chill in my undies!! Much to my surprise (and relief!), my friend replied, "OMG! I totally get those days. No worries. Just let me know when else we can meet" – and that was the end of that! Nobody got upset. Nobody shouted. She didn't stop being my friend. And the world wasn't over! Plus, I didn't have to keep up some ridiculous white lie about whatever I had *said* I was doing at the time. Bonus!

Admittedly, this is a pretty simple example of saying no. Yet it's a scenario that's so common we're likely to come up against it again and again in our lives. I started to see that, at some point, I had convinced myself that not being available for other people 24/7 made me a bad person! But it doesn't, of course! There's absolutely nothing wrong with creating some regular time all to yourself when you can manage it!

My top tips for starting to say no are:

- **Start small.** This is a learning curve, so it's best not to say no to huge things straightaway. Instead, it's good to gradually get used to saying no to little things; then move on from there when you feel ready.
- **Remember you have a choice.** It's easy to feel obligated out of duty to say "yes" to other people all the time, but you always have a choice – even if it doesn't feel like it!
- **No excuses.** It's easy to feel that you need to explain yourself, or justify your "no" to others, but you don't owe this courtesy to anyone.

- **Stand firm.** If you say no, don't then let someone try and persuade you, or guilt trip you, into changing your mind. Standing firm in your initial response will set a precedent that makes it easier to manage this boundary in the future.
- **Don't fear the fall out.** Not everyone is going to like you saying no, especially if you've just started, but there's no need to fear! You are *not* doing anything wrong and it's ok that some people may not like it. The people who have benefited most from your previous lack of boundaries will be the ones who are likely to find the transition the hardest. But that's *their* issue, not yours.

Make Time for Yourself

Getting time on my own isn't easy these days, what with being a married, working Mum. I have work commitments, a husband, the kids and the pets who all need and want my time.

But if we're *constantly* surrounded by others, the tendency is to become consumed by what *they* say and do, to focus only on *their* needs, to take on *their* energy, and to absorb any negativity that they may be bringing to the table.

It's therefore of utmost importance to make time for *ourselves*, too – and not to feel guilty that this time isn't being used "productively". It really *is* ok to have time by yourself, even if you're doing nothing. Rest is as important as hustle, as only when we feel restored, refuelled and recharged can we provide for others from a place of abundance and overflow, rather than from our reserve tank.

There are so many benefits to regular time to yourself. It gives you space to switch off, to relax, to breathe deeply, to realign with the things that are most important to you, and generally to get to know yourself better, so that you can then put your best, most authentic self forward.

Having valuable time alone also gives you increased head space so that you can have more empathy and compassion for others, which is particularly key if the opinions of the people around you are sometimes negative and not in line with how you want to be.

We often present slightly different versions of ourselves depending on where we are and who we're with. My Mum, for example, has a "posh" phone voice at work; I remember going to the office with her one time as a child and wondering who the calm, collected, super professional woman was! It's totally natural for us to do things like this but if we do it *all* the time, it can become difficult to then really understand who we are at our core. Having time by ourselves helps to counteract this by allowing us to "just be", without any outside influence, which will lead to us reconnecting with your innermost authentic self. Hurrah!

Say "I Don't Want to Talk About it"

Conversation boundaries are great. They have been one of the ways that I have really protected myself from getting into debates and confrontations that I don't want to be in – with people that I don't want to be in them with.

Just to be clear ... this is not to say that I'm only happy to take part in conversations with people whose beliefs are the same as mine, as I don't believe that any of us would get very far in life if we all took this approach! However, we are well within our rights to determine certain conversations that we'd rather not take part in at certain times – and how we would like to manage these.

I was recently in a group setting where the conversation turned to a subject that I'm not comfortable discussing publicly and actually find quite triggering. The person leading the group insisted that everyone get involved, asking us all to raise a hand and take it in turns to discuss our experience. I could feel the anxiety racing through me, a sickness creeping up from the pit of my stomach, and I was physically shaking waiting for my name to be called. I *really* didn't want to be part of the conversation, but every person in the group of 14 was getting involved, so I would be the only person *not* to.

I was berating myself in my head: "Just speak up. It's no big deal! Why are you creating so much drama?! Everyone else is getting involved, so why not you too?". In so doing, I now realize that I was invalidating my own feelings by trying to make out that I was just being "ridiculous" and that I should get "over myself".

Thankfully, I was able to stop myself, take a breath, drown out the noise of everyone else talking just for a moment, and tune into my gut. And as soon as I did this, I knew that if I wanted to really step into my power, I needed to Own the way I felt and give myself permission to step away from the conversation (which I knew was going to do me more harm than good in that moment).

When my name was called, I therefore simply said, "Thank you but this isn't a conversation I feel comfortable discussing at the moment." Boom! I had done it! My heart was racing at a million beats a minute and I felt like a superhero – until, that is, the person leading responded with the statement, "It really isn't that big of a deal Jess. Everyone else has shared, so it's only fair."

Now, if she had been talking to Jess a few years before, I would have ignored all my blaring sirens telling me to stick up for myself and stand my ground. I would have given in. And I would have really regretted it afterward. But I decided that this time was going to be different. This time I was not just representing Jess *now*; I was holding my own for all the times I hadn't done so before – for all the times I had said or done something that I wasn't comfortable doing just because I wanted to be seen as a good, helpful, co-operative person! And let me tell you, when you get into this mindset of not just sticking up for your *current* self but also for your *past* self, there really is nothing that will stop you.

I responded, "It's great that everyone felt happy to share, but this isn't something I wish to discuss further at the moment. I'm happy to take this conversation outside of the group to discuss, but, for now, I'm going to remove myself from the conversation and return when I feel it's safe to do so." Mic drop.

There is something so incredible about showing up for yourself in this way – for standing so strong in the boundaries that you have set to protect yourself. Nobody can argue with you when you're factual, firm and forward. That moment has stayed with me ever since, and continues to prove to me the utmost importance of *upholding* boundaries that you want to have in place so that you can, ultimately, control more of your own narrative in life.

KNOWING WHEN TO LEAVE

I read a quote once that said, "Knowing when to leave is the most important thing. Whether it's the job, the relationship or the party." It made me think about just how vital leaving at the right time is in order to avoid all sorts of negative interactions, situations or people.

Just think – if we hadn't left the people, situations, jobs and relationships that we have already left in the past, we wouldn't be where we are today. And, no matter how low you may feel in moments in your current situation, you always have the opportunity to change things and/or start afresh by leaving behind certain aspects of your current life.

When I reflect back on past circumstances, I realize that I often instinctively knew quite soon into certain situations that I should move on from them for my own good. But I often didn't step away straightaway because I was afraid of the consequences – of the pain or disappointment, for example, that I would cause for either myself and/or others. A good lesson from this is to learn to "trust your instincts" more. But it's also important to look out for signs in the way you might be feeling that tell you it's time to end a relationship. Two of the main signs for me have often been when I've realized that:

- I'm feeling a need to shrink and hide away in the relationship by making myself "small"

and/or

- I'm feeling like I'm just "too much" for the other person or people

Neither of these are nice ways to feel so let's delve into them a little further to find out more ...

You Make Yourself Small

I have spent a lot of time in my life trying to "make myself small" in the physical sense (incessantly trying to lose weight, as per the "fat" part of "The Fat Funny One" persona). But I've also done it in a lot of other ways – trying to shrink myself down to invisibility, dampen my personality or make myself fade into the background – all in order to make *others* feel more comfortable.

If you constantly feel like this within a particular relationship, it's a strong sign that you probably shouldn't stay in that situation for much longer. However, walking away can be difficult in circumstances where the relationship ties are tight (for example, if it's your parents and you live with them, or a friend who you see daily). In cases like this, it's good to at least start creating safe boundaries (see page 128) in order to protect yourself and support your journey to self-love and Owning It.

One example of me being in a situation where I used to try to make myself smaller (in the metaphorical sense) was in a job where my boss was constantly putting me down, undermining my decision-making and generally making sure that "I knew my place". I thought I was handling it pretty well at the time – managing to keep things contained in order to "keep the peace". But in suppressing my authentic self to try to keep the peace with her, what I didn't realize is that I was starting a war inside myself – fighting against who I really was! And what's the point of that!?

I am a fairly talkative person (surprise!). I love being sociable, asking people about themselves and just connecting with people in any social setting, including within the workplace. Around the table at a team lunch one day, we were all chatting away and enjoying getting to know one another a little better (it was all paid for by the company and who doesn't love a free lunch!). On our return to the office, my manager called me in, sat me down and told me that she was "sick of listening" to me talking and that she knew that my colleagues felt the same. She advised me that it was therefore in my best interest to keep quiet.

I was devastated. I truly felt like I had been kicked in the stomach because I thought I had been getting along with everyone so well. But I took the advice and tried to keep myself to myself. I didn't engage in conversations even when invited into them. I would make cups of tea when others weren't in the kitchen to avoid connecting with anyone. And I just put my head down and worked! I thought this was the best thing to do while in the office – and that I could then be my friendly, chatty self again when I went home each evening. But I was wrong!

We spend so much time at work – often more time than we get at home with our families or enjoying free time. And so ... the behaviour that I had adopted at work started to seep into all areas of my life. I became a shadow of the chatty, sociable person I was before, and I found myself avoiding invitations to go out with friends, not having full conversations with people, and avoiding asking people about themselves – all because I was so used to behaving this way at work! I had become a version of myself that neither I, nor my friends and family recognized any more.

I knew that I needed to remove myself from this work situation as soon as I could – to find a way of returning to my true self. But I also knew that leaving straightaway wasn't an option. And, unfortunately, I didn't know then what I know now: that there were also various ways to *manage* a situation like this in order to limit the damaging effect on me.

Some of the approaches that I gradually learned are:

- **Keep it simple.** Looking back, I often replay in my head some of the conversations I've had and wish I had been more direct with my responses to uphold my boundaries where I could. Instead, I often allowed my emotions to get in the way of my communications so would over-explain myself, as if trying to justify things. When dealing with someone who you want to create distance from, it's best to keep communication clear and simple, leaving no room for them to over-communicate their frustrations with you. No emotive language like "I feel ...". Just short, simple, matter-of-fact answers.

- **Seek support.** Confide in someone else about what is happening and, if you need to, take someone as support with you when dealing with the person or people who are making you feel "less than". When I felt bullied by a midwife throughout my first pregnancy, I started taking my partner with me to appointments. He could then advocate for me when I didn't feel strong enough or needed reinforcement.

- **Minimize your exposure.** If you don't need to be around the person making you feel small, then don't be!

This isn't about awkwardly avoiding every interaction; it's about establishing a reasonable time limit on how long you feel you can be around them. For example, maybe being with your family is fine for up to an hour but gets uncomfortable after that? Moving forward, it could therefore be useful to set yourself this hour time limit for your next visit, maybe even setting an alarm on your phone to remind you when it's time to say your goodbyes.

- **Plan your responses.** I often used to walk away from situations kicking myself for not having given a kick-ass comeback, so now, when I know that I'm going to be around someone potentially problematic to me, I have a few pre-empted responses up my sleeve. Don't get me wrong, I don't have a script that I memorize. I just establish in my own head whether there are topics that I would prefer to stay away from, and if so, how I'll handle that. For example, I had a friend who always loved to discuss relationships and boast about how great hers was – even if mine wasn't at the time! So if she asked me how things were on that front, I'd just say, "Oh I'm not talking about that tonight. Let's talk about you! How's work?" Throwing the focus of the question back to her in this way really helped me to feel more in control and manage the emotions of the situation better.

You Feel Like You're "Too Much"

I've spent a lot of my life telling myself that I am too this, too that and too the other thing (too loud, too chatty, too bossy, too quiet, too stupid, too fat …) – rather than embracing and Owning *all* the beautiful parts of myself that make me who I am.

When you feel *too* anything it can cause havoc with you reaching your potential, learning to love yourself and feeling content. This is because many of us are taught that it's not a good thing to be *too much* of anything – even when the characteristic is something positive, like being clever!

Many of these deep-rooted feelings about ourselves will come from notions that we have developed and held onto since childhood, so these will need to be worked through when breaking down and reframing our limiting beliefs (see Chapter 1).

The most significant reframing in this area for me, which has really helped me to gain a new appreciation of the things that I once deemed as negative, was the realization that being "too much" of something can actually be viewed as an amazing gift, rather than as a fault or weakness!!

Below are examples of some of my long-held "too much" beliefs that I have reframed as precious gifts over the years:

- I'm too nerdy ⟶ I have the gift of seeking out knowledge and loving learning
- I'm too emotional ⟶ I have the gift of being able to feel things deeply
- I'm too bossy ⟶ I have the gift of being assertive and leading strongly
- I'm too quiet ⟶ I have the gift of being a thoughtful and considered listener
- I'm just generally too much ⟶ I have the gift of confidence to be who I am abundantly and unapologetically

It is so important that you see your own gifts in yourself, recognize that they contribute to your greatness, and Own them without fear of judgement from others.

You'll know that you've found great people to spend your time with when they embrace, support and love *all* of you, when you feel entirely comfortable just being yourself with them, and when you don't feel like you're ever being "too much" of anything. Because you're not! You're bloody fabulous!

REFRAMING THE F WORD (FAILURE)

When we make a decision to walk away from certain situations in our lives, we often see the breaking of ties as a failing. If we have to leave a relationship, we might feel that we "failed" at being a good partner. If we have to leave a job, we might feel it's because we "failed" at being an effective team member. The list is endless. But the feeling of "failure" is not helpful for anyone, and, in my humble opinion, needs to be completely reframed.

There is a famous saying that goes: "You have only failed if you didn't learn something" – and I believe this to be true. Personally, I can't think of any scenario that I have ever been in where I haven't learned something, which, based on this quote, means that there's no such thing as failure. Boom!

It's crucial to understand that just because something hasn't worked out in the way you planned, expected or hoped it would, doesn't mean that you or anyone else has failed. Change is one of the only things that is guaranteed in this world, which means that people and circumstances change all the time. So it's ok – and, some might argue, partially to be expected! – that some things do not quite work out as planned. It's therefore best to try not to let yourself get sucked into believing that you have "failed" at anything in life. In my eyes, you haven't! You are simply learning what works and what doesn't, and are shaping your strengths and skillsets, so that you know how to do things better next time.

DEALING WITH BEING BULLIED

The common definition of "bullying" describes it as "repeated behaviour with intention to cause someone pain and hurt, either physically or emotionally". According to the 2018 bullying survey by global youth charity Ditch the Label, 1.5 million young people were bullied in 2017–2018 in the UK alone, 57% of these identifying as female. But the problem is by no means isolated to the UK. According to a 2019 study by Pacer National Bullying Prevention Centre, 29% of young people aged 18 and younger in the US reported being bullied. And what is even more scary is that 13% of younger teens (aged 9–12) reported being bullied in school, home or online.

When we think about bullying, we often think of a school setting. This is the most common place for people to experience bullying in their lifetime. My personal experience of being bullied was different because, although I had a few run-ins of that kind during my school years, the real, soul-destroying bullying happened to me when I was an adult, at work!

Bullying has such a deep impact on those involved. It often leaves people scared, embarrassed, lacking in confidence and questioning their self-worth. There is no question that it changes the courses of many people's lives and, in some cases, can sadly make people want to no longer live theirs.

It is often said to those who are bullied that the person doing the bullying tends to be in some kind of internal pain themselves (which is what's causing them to act in such a horrible way). But, let's be honest, when you're suffering at the hands of the bullies, it's hard to comprehend, or even care, because your priority is to want the pain to stop for *you*.

One of the questions I asked myself time and time again when being bullied in the workplace was, "What did I do to deserve this?" I tried for a long time to figure this out. The why! *Why* did people feel the need to treat me this badly? *Why* couldn't they just leave me alone? With hindsight, I can now see that I was focusing on the why because I wanted to be able to understand and therefore maybe control it. I felt that if I knew why, then maybe I would be able to *change* whatever it was so that they would like me. Maybe they would treat me fairly. And maybe I wouldn't have to deal with the pain ...

Whether negativity and bullying are showing up in a very direct way in your life or in more subtle ways, such as flippant comments from friends that hurt your feelings or negative comments from strangers that do the same, the end result is the same: wounding and pain.

I was unable to stop the bullying that happened at my workplace. I was unable to click my fingers and make it go away, or control what the *other* people involved were doing. In the end, I just had to get the hell out of Dodge. Since then, I have learned about various actions that I could have taken to help me while still in the situation – and which I will hope will help you, as you move forward on your journey! These are:

- Share it with someone
- Acknowledge it's not you
- Stay connected
- Identify your next steps
- Keep being a good person

Let's explore each of these a little more ...

Share it with Someone

Being targeted and bullied can bring so much shame that it can make it difficult to feel like you can tell anyone about it without being seen as dramatic or overreacting. There can also be a lot of fear that saying something might make the situation worse. But there is honestly so much power in speaking out and telling someone that you trust about it. Whether that person is able to support you by taking action to help stop the bullying, or they are able to simply provide you with a safe space for you to voice what's happening, saying out loud what is happening is key to being able to start getting the help that you need.

Acknowledge it's Not You

The "Why me?" thoughts are likely to be hard to shift, but acknowledging that there's nothing you have done wrong and that you do *not* deserve this negative treatment will help you in knowing that you are worthy of getting support to make things stop. Nobody deserves to be bullied, ridiculed or treated badly, and everyone has the right to feel safe, loved and respected. Repeat after me: "It's not my fault! It's not my fault! It's not my fault!"

Stay Connected

Staying connected to both people and activities that make you feel good and fill you with joy is an important act of self-care, particularly when you're going through hard times that may be affecting your mental, emotional and physical health. Many negative interactions or instances of bullying make you feel isolated and lonely, so it's essential that you can maintain being connected to what you love, with a sense of goodness in your life.

Identify Your Next Steps

This may sound strange, but it's important to identify the *type* of bully that you are dealing with in any given circumstance. In most cases, we are unlikely to want to continue a relationship with the person causing us the trouble (if there ever was one in the first place) because of the way they have been treating us. But, in some cases, we may want to try to repair the relationship and move forward. If this is the case, try to gently open the doors of communication and start the conversation. It is unlikely to be easy, but if it's important to you, then you *deserve* to have an open, honest conversation about how someone else is making you feel.

Keep Being a Good Person

It sounds obvious, but the reality of remaining kind-hearted when people are being very unkind takes a great deal of resilience – a strength that you may not even know you have until you are in the situation. Thoughts of retaliation and "What's the point in being kind?" might sometimes float around in your head. But it's important to never stop being a good person because of a bad person (or people).

Many people will try to dim, or even put out, the light you have inside of you as you travel on your brave journey to self-love – and you may even feel like letting that light extinguish at times, as relief from the stress and pain that you are going through. But your light is what keeps you *you*. Your light is what others need. Your goodness and kindness will, in the end, positively impact others in the world so beautifully. And both you, and the incredible people who have the opportunity to *experience* you, deserve to see that light and bask in the glow of the authentic confidence and joy that emanate from it.

IT'S NOT YOUR BURDEN TO CARRY

When someone has an issue with you, or your behaviour or an aspect of who you are, it's important to know that it's not *your* burden to carry, but theirs. This works the other way too, so if there's something about another person that *you* don't like or that makes *you* feel jealous or frustrated, it's often something that *you* are holding on to causing the problem.

Understanding this has changed my life. It has allowed me to not take on the pressure or weight of other people's opinions – whether good or bad. And it has allowed me to move forward more freely, with only the weight of my own thoughts on my shoulders.

We must create a world where the kindest, loudest and most important voice we hear is our own; if we live by the validation and opinions of others, we will starve ourselves of so much joy and freedom that we will essentially be depriving ourselves of truly living.

Some of the key questions that I therefore now ask myself when I'm hit with negative feedback are:

- "Is this personal?"
- "Is it *really* about me?"
- "And even if it *is* about me ... is it *true*?"

Just because it is being typed or said out loud, and has your name linked to it, doesn't mean there's any truth to it!

I can, hand on heart (with full conviction), tell you that, had I continued to listen to the negative talk from all the "mean girls", naysayers, bullies and people who just wanted to throw their two cents worth in along my journey, I would not be here, living the life that I'm now living, or writing this book. I would not be in the job I'm in. I would not be in a loving relationship with my husband. And I would not get such pure joy every single day from my beautiful children and fur babies.

I often reflect on the enormity of this – the fact that, had I not just got myself out of my hole of self-loathing and gone for it, I wouldn't even have known that the life I'm now happily living was *possible* – never mind have the privilege of *living* it!

As I write this now, I ask you not to put yourself in the position of one day looking back and wondering what joy you, too, could have had if only you had gone for it and decided to Own It (instead of letting the mean girls and naysayers win!).

I can tell you from personal experience that you can't even imagine the potential for your life right now. Things can be even better than in your wildest dreams if you take this chance to step into your power by disconnecting from all the negative talk.

Doing what you need to do for *you* first and foremost will *always* be the best decision that you make. And for anyone who can't see this or doesn't want to acknowledge your greatness, there's always the block button!

Owning It Top Tip

When something happens that upsets you or winds you up, make a conscious choice to do a Taylor Swift and "shake it off". Changing your attitude to focus on what joy you can feel in the moment will help to loosen the grip of the negative narrative.

THROWING A BLOCK PARTY

My "block" button gets pressed pretty often these days (seriously, there's a whole block party going on at my place!) Don't get me wrong, I try my best, where possible, to just filter out the negative. But the reality is that the Internet is anyone's game, so, no matter how hard I try, there will always be something that comes up that triggers me and that I'll find difficult to shake. Sometimes these messages aren't blatant name-calling and abuse; they might even be neatly wrapped in "niceness" and privilege, presented as "concern" or "advice" (yet be deeply patronizing or passive aggressive beneath the surface!)

While blocking is a great tool to have on social media, it doesn't *always* solve the problem. And obviously, it isn't as easy as just "blocking" people when you have to deal with them in "real life".

So how can you stop the real-life people from saying damaging things and hurting you? When I started looking into how I could do this, I felt pretty damn frustrated with the advice that I found; and I expect you may be a little, too, by the time you get to the end of the paragraph, because, unfortunately, there simply *is* no way of stopping people wanting to give their "important" opinions and pour salt on other people's wounds!

I think there are three main reasons that people generally feel so free to share their negative opinions of you – whether directly to you or via others:

- A deep-rooted self-loathing leads to a projection of their negative view about themselves onto others
- Perpetuating the programmed idea that people should be judged and that they have the entitlement to do that, whether on physical appearance, on how people choose to identify or on anything else
- Probably the most irritating reason of them all – some people are just jerks

Now, in no way am I calling anyone reading this book a jerk (I mean, the fact that you're reading my book means that you're pretty bloody awesome), but I am certain that many of us have had moments in our lives where we, too, have been negative about someone else – whether we made assumptions about their character, judged the way they present themselves based on our *own* perception of what life should be, or projected our own insecurities onto them. Most of us have been there at some point or another, and it doesn't make us bad people! It simply makes us human! But what will stop us from reaching full jerk status is self-awareness – simply noticing where we might be starting to spill into a negative, "judgey" head space about ourselves or someone else, catching ourselves and pulling ourselves back in line – so that we can feel more fulfilled, more whole and happier in who we are.

Self-Reflection Questions

On Dealing with "Mean Girls" & Naysayers

- Am I heavily influenced by what others say about me or expect of me?
- Do I need to set more boundaries to stop others from influencing me so negatively?
- What relationships are not adding value to my life right now?
- Do I have people who I can go to for support, both in good times and bad?
- Do I need to reach out for more support to deal with any current negative issues?
- What could my life be like if I didn't care about what anyone else said?

GUIDED TASK
Reframing Your "Too Much"

Are there elements of yourself that you've been repeatedly told are "too much" (as discussed on page 140) and/or that you feel worried or anxious about within yourself? If so, this is an opportunity for you to identify any such feelings and reframe them into something more positive that will allow you to feel much better within yourself.

What To Do

1. Take a few moments to identify any feelings of "too muchness" in your life at the moment and write them down. For example, I've been told or thought at times in my life that:

   - I'm too chatty
   - I'm too controlling
   - I'm too detail-oriented

2. Challenge yourself to turn each of these "too much" beliefs into a statement that reframes the same quality as a gift, or special talent, that you are grateful for. For example:

- I'm too chatty ⎯⎯➤ I have the gift of being able to communicate & connect well with people
- I'm too controlling ⎯⎯➤ I have the gift of being able to organize and lead things well
- I'm too detail-oriented ⎯⎯➤ I have the gift of seeing a level of things that other people don't always see

See also page 141 for further examples of "too much" statements that have been reframed into "gift" statements.

3. When you've finished, put your reframed statements somewhere that you can refer back to – so that the next time someone says something that leads to you feeling like you're "too much" of something, you can use them to reframe their hurtful words with a more positive outlook.

Chapter 5

Embracing Your Body & Loving the Skin You're In

"Nothing tastes as good as skinny feels" was a famous quote in 2009 from British model Kate Moss. Causing somewhat of a sensation at the time (as well as a controversy!), this quote went on to be used as marketing for just about every slimming club going for quite some time after (and even some to this day). At the time, I really believed it, because *of course* happiness and success would come when I eventually got to my goal weight (which for me meant being "skinny")! And *of course* that was when I would start living my life!

It makes me shudder just thinking about it now! There is just so much wrong with the statement that I'm surprised it was allowed to be used so freely.

Whether you are plus size, big-boned, slim, petite, tall, athletic, skinny or any other shape or size on the spectrum, you are entitled to feel however you *want* about your own body. Kate Moss's statement – and the many other similar beliefs that are still out there today – makes those who *aren't* skinny feel like they *should* be, and those who *are* skinny feel wrong if they don't feel *good*. And none of this is positive for *anyone* in *any* body.

Regardless of your shape or size: you deserve to feel good about the skin you're in, and the body that carries you around each day. The body that is enabling you to read or listen to this book, that enabled you to get out of bed this morning, have that refreshing shower and get on with the day's activities. It took me a long time to realize that I deserve to feel good about my incredible body. But I am so glad that I did at least realize it in the end, because no good was ever going to come from chasing beauty standards that aren't realistic and a body ideal that often isn't even real.

Have you ever looked back at old photos and thought "Wow! I thought I was fat then!"? – only to realize that you actually looked nothing *like* you thought you had at the time!? Insights like this are all the evidence I need to show me that our own body image has very *little* to do with our bodies at all and *very much* to do with our minds.

I often now find myself looking back at those same old photos, wondering how on earth I saw anything other than a beautiful, vibrant woman in them. It's been eye-opening for me to realize just how very much my negative thoughts and limiting beliefs impacted the experience of what I physically saw in my own reflection in years gone by!

A LIFE OF DIETING

I genuinely don't think that there's a diet I haven't tried. I've counted calories, attended classes and clubs, taken pills to suppress hunger, drank disgusting powdered shakes and even ate only baby food at one point (yeah, I know!). There has been fasting – completely, intermittently and 5:2 (I've tried them all!). Yet despite each approach being so different, the outcome was always the same for me: an emotional rollercoaster after which I was left feeling full of guilt and shame.

Every time would start the same: I would be excited about the programme and think of all the things I would do once I got to my goal. I would buy everything associated with the plan – from the branded food and magazines to the food diaries and stickers! You name it, I "needed" it (because we all know that pretty stickers stop you eating cake!). I would then completely immerse myself in the regime of the moment, I would do it all perfectly, and bam, week one = a few pounds off.

Stepping on the scales always felt like a huge moment – as if time stood still. I remember the overwhelming anxiety that I would feel, because if I hadn't even lost a bean when I had stuck so closely to the plan, then what would the point have been?

One of my top priorities when joining a weight loss group was to find a group that had sessions in the morning, because apparently you weigh less in the morning! When it wasn't possible, and I had to find one after work, I would spend the whole day eating as little as possible to stay as "light" as I could. I'd then worry the whole day about whether or not that little box on the floor was going to tell me I was worth something or not. Even if I had done truly amazing things in other areas of my life, none of it mattered because all my sense of achievement was tied up at that time in getting a number lower on the scales than the week before.

I would often feel physically sick about getting weighed and do a sneaky weigh-in during the week to see if I could estimate how proud or disappointed I would be when weigh day came around. Looking back, I realize just how much it dominated every aspect of my life. That small box, which simply took a measurement of my body, was ruling my life.

After doing the rounds of the different diets, I finally settled on one where you had to count something called "syns". It seemed like the one diet where I could eat carbs, and I certainly didn't want to give *those* up! Although the group was after work (disappointing), it was only round the corner from my house and was at a handy time, so this meant I could go on my way home and then finally eat something substantial before 7pm.

Now, if you've never been to a weight loss group, then let me break down what happens. You arrive and everyone stands in a queue to get weighed, one by one. Someone writes down your results in your weight loss diary and you then take a seat. Once everyone is weighed it turns into a kind of mini award ceremony, where certificates are handed out to those who have hit milestones or lost the most weight, while everyone else claps them on. Then, once this is finished, the leader goes round the group and asks people to discuss their losses, including why they did so well that week, or why (like me most weeks) they *hadn't* done so well!

BULLYING MYSELF SKINNY

When I would have a "bad week", I would punish myself harshly. I would look at my body in the mirror and purposefully point out all of the negative things that I saw. I would eat less, weigh myself more and, at one point, I even set a picture of myself that I hated as my phone screensaver, as well as printing a copy to put on the fridge door – to deter myself from eating. It didn't work!

For over a decade, I lived on this seemingly endless rollercoaster of losing a little weight and feeling on top of the world, then gaining or maintaining weight and feeling as though I was a complete failure. But at some point, I finally started to become aware of just how much I was hating on myself and the fact that I was *never* going to be able to "punish myself "into being skinny!

Up until then, I seemed to think that if I was frustrated or angry enough at myself, it would ignite the hidden diet-lover and "skinny girl" in me – and everything would change! Unsurprisingly, however, the immense pressure that I was putting on myself *wasn't* motivating me to do anything differently. It was just making me feel more and more horrible about myself.

I now know, after years of research, that it's having *positive* thoughts about yourself – and truly *loving* yourself – that can bring about the most change. And sometimes, I find myself wishing that I had found this out sooner!

I know that the whole notion of "positive thinking" can come across as fluffy, "silly" and overly simplistic to many. However, there is real science that confirms its power.

Barbara Fredrickson, a professor of Psychology and Neuroscience at the University of North Carolina at Chapel Hill, is one of many who have carried out extensive research into this topic. Among her significant findings has been how negative emotions greatly *narrow* our thinking, placing our focus only on the "bad" and therefore making it difficult for us to feel hopeful or happy. She explained that negative emotions tend to be so strong and emotive (normally connecting with deep-rooted angers, hurts or frustrations), that we're unable to see a feasible path *away* from them. Instead, we become all-consumed by them, which can all too easily snowball into much deeper and darker places if we're not careful. Fredrickson also wrote about the hugely beneficial effect that *positive* thoughts can have on us, and is well-known for the "broaden-and-build" theory in particular, which affirms just what a fundamental role positive emotions, such as joy, interest, contentment and love, play in our lives in terms of giving us the tools for successful coping and survival.

ENOUGH IS ENOUGH

My constant attempts at dieting meant that I was at war with myself. I obsessed over everything. I didn't socialize because I was too afraid of having no self-control and going over my "daily allowance" (of food that is!). It was all-consuming. But my turning point – and the end of my days of unhappy dieting – was when my eldest daughter, Sophia, only three years old at the time, asked me if she was fat, and refused to eat anything – just like I was doing!

Only then did I discover that, despite having spent years obsessively reading the back of every packet of food I bought, looking at calorie calculators and studying recipes, I had no real understanding about nutrition or what was really good for my body. I had convinced myself that the diet industry wanted me to feel better, *be* better and make all these wonderful lifestyle changes for myself. But, in actual fact, they had taught me more often than not that a meal that came out of a sachet and needed a microwave to be cooked was a better choice than an avocado! It seemed much more concerned about making me "smaller" than "better" – and, ideally, a repeat customer in the process!

Now I want to be crystal clear here – I'm not talking about the health sector, which is a different thing entirely. I'm talking about the multi-billion pound diet industry that thrives solely off us wanting to change the way we look! It's only when I stepped away from my unhealthy obsession with this world that I realized just how messed up it all really is. I had spent years immersed in it, yet the only parts of me that had gotten any "smaller" were my self-worth and my bank balance!

I wish I had known earlier (obviously) the huge difference that stopping the incessant diets would make to my mental health. My focus had always been on *what* I saw in the mirror, rather than *who* I saw. I was so fixated on looks – whether mine or that of others – that I was caught in a vicious cycle of judgement and shaming. I was completely obsessed with what everyone else was wearing, eating, doing and looking like because it was my only way of defining my *own* worth, and therefore also my only way of determining that of others.

I was full-blown projecting my insecurities on everyone around me. I disliked and was threatened by those who I deemed more beautiful or acceptable by societal standards. And I harshly judged those who I deemed to have the same issues that I was facing myself.

Let me tell you about a time that I full-on negatively projected onto someone else. There was a group of us who were all pretty close, and we had arranged a boozy night out. Once we had finally set a date on which we all agreed (an epic task in itself for seven women), we started to discuss what to wear. One of the group was a friend of a friend so someone we weren't as close to, but we often saw each other at nights out and for mutual friends' birthdays and the like. Let's call her Maria.

Maria is a beautiful plus-size woman who was extremely confident, and a total fashionista. I would always have this underlying feeling that I didn't quite like her. I had no idea why but something about her bothered me.

Anyway, back to the planning of our girls' night out ... We all started discussing clothes and sending one another pictures of ourselves in potential outfits to help us decide what to wear; jeans and a nice top wouldn't cut it on this occasion. And, as part of this, Maria sent pictures of herself in a body-con dress, which showed every lady lump and bump that she had. I instantly found myself judging her for wearing clothes that were "inappropriate" for her size! I couldn't understand why anyone would want to purposefully show off their tummy, back rolls and jiggly bits, rather than wear something more "flattering", like one of the outfits that I had chosen – black, baggy and entirely "suitable" for someone plus size, like me, to hide themselves in!

I now know that not a single one of those critical thoughts about Maria were because of *anything* that Maria wore or did: they had absolutely *nothing* to do with her, and *everything* to do with me. Without me realizing it, seeing Maria in her fabulous, figure-hugging dress had brought out my own insecurities and jealousy about the fact that *I* wouldn't have had the confidence to wear anything as fabulous and figure-hugging at the time! And this led to me projecting on to Maria my fear of showing my *own* body (tummy 'n' all!) in clothes that I actually liked (rather than what the world deemed as "size appropriate")! I was so deep into diet culture – and conforming to society's standards – that I had allowed myself to fall into a pattern of judging other incredible women!

When you're plus size you get used to being constantly judged, commented on, frowned upon and tutted at by others – and to hating that! Yet here I was judging someone else in exactly the same way!

It was only once I started to confront my own body image issues that I realized my judgement of Maria was actually about an internal battle that I was having with myself. And, while I can safely say from my own experience and exposure that this kind of internal battle is a common issue for many plus-size women, I have learned from my wider contacts that it is also very common among women all of *all* shapes and sizes, including women who are seen as "skinny" (as they often have to endure comments about them not eating enough and being unhealthy, etc).

It seems like you simply can't win unless you look like the cover of a magazine and even then, there will be a fair few people who will have something negative to say about that!

WHAT YOU SEE IS WHAT YOU GET

Many people seem surprised when they meet me that I'm only five-foot-two (1.57m). However, that is where my petiteness ends! As I mentioned near the start of the book, I'm a size 18 (UK) woman, who has had three children. I have a big bust, stretch marks, cellulite and plenty of wobbly bits – most of which have pretty close relationships with gravity.

Two years after I had started up The Fat Funny One, and had really began to discover what confidence meant and looked like for me, I took the bold step of entering a competition hosted by lingerie brand Curvy Kate, called "Star in a Bra". They were looking for regular women to feature in their upcoming shoot for the next season's styles. The shoot and the brand were about celebrating real women and real bodies – so I wanted to be part of it, and sent off my headshots and details. Much to my surprise, I was invited to the next stage of auditions, which was a lingerie shoot in London. I remember how over the moon I was on the day I got the email telling me – but I also instantly had a pang of regret and anxiety because this meant that I was actually going to have to get my kit off in front of real people!

On the day of the shoot I went to London and felt physically sick. I mean it was one thing imagining the shoot – but actually doing it!? My goodness! I was fitted with my lingerie by the most fantastic bra whizz called Chantelle, and I had my make-up done professionally. I was handed a nice robe to wear and was feeling wonderful – until, that is, it was my turn to shoot and the nerves kicked in.

What I hadn't realized was that the room would be filled with all the other women taking part that day too; there were ten other women ready to take part. Some were plus-size models, others novices like me, but *all* absolutely amazing. Every single body was different. Big boobs, small boobs, pert boobs, saggy boobs, cellulite, big thighs, small thighs and everything in between.

I looked around the room in absolute awe of how incredible everyone looked and just how diverse a woman's body could be. At one point in the day we were sitting around talking, and it reminded me of when you're drunk in nightclub toilets and have a compliment battle with a random stranger who ends up becoming your best mate. We were all throwing each other positive feedback and telling one another what was so amazing about the other. I asked one of the more experienced models how she had the confidence to even start this journey, and how she copes with it all. And she simply said: "What you see is what you get". A simple statement, but a strong and effective one to live by!

EMBRACING OUR BODIES AS THEY ARE

I appreciate that not everyone is going to do something as extreme as enter a lingerie competition, and, to be honest, it was a pretty bold step to make even for me. But there are so many other ways in which you can take small steps toward feeling more comfortable in your own skin (without having to get your kit off!). Your journey doesn't have to look like mine, but it does have to begin somewhere!

One small but significant way to start is to make a decision to wear something that you've always wanted to try but have feared to up until now. This might be a pair of shorts (that shows off your usually well-hidden legs), it might be a more fitted top than usual, it might be a dress like Maria's, or it might just be something in a brighter, bolder colour than normal. Any and all of these things would be valid steps toward becoming more confident in your own body.

For me, the lingerie competition was a catalyst for starting to post more pictures of my body online. I wanted other women, who were happily scrolling on my site, to experience the same kind of inspirational impact that seeing the incredible diverse bodies of other women at the photoshoot had had on me! I wanted women to see bodies that weren't all like the ones on the cover of almost every magazine; to feel inspired, and to be filled with a sense of acceptance about themselves. I shared pictures of my body *reality* because I wanted others to know that *their* bodies were incredible too, just as they were.

While the majority of the reactions to my pictures were positive and achieved what I hoped, a fair chunk (pun intended) of people suddenly became medical professionals and believed they could assess my health based solely on what I looked like. I remember one woman saying that she was sure she knew my exact BMI (Body Mass Index; a measure of value derived from the mass or weight and height of a person) from just one picture that she had seen of me, in a bikini, on Facebook.

If it wasn't a comment about the diabetes (that I don't have), the strain on my very strong and happy knees, or (believe it or not!) being told that I deserved to die and have my children taken away from me, then it was unoriginal slurs about being fat. I'm not saying everyone should *like* my body, of course, and I'm always happy to have open discussions with whoever about whatever – including engaging in constructive debates – however, I shouldn't be abused because of my body; no one should.

No negative comments or criticisms are easy to read, but for a long time I took them in willingly – because they affirmed all of the negative beliefs that I already had about my body. Despite being on the start of this incredible journey to self-love, all of my horrible insecurities came creeping back to the surface. But this time, rather than sit with these negative feelings and allowing myself to become consumed by them, I decided to make another decision – to become more informed. I wanted to *understand* all the things that I was frightened of and know what these various medical terms that people were throwing at me really meant ...

BMI BS

When pregnant with my second daughter, Isabella, I went to my doctor's surgery after suffering quite severe stomach pains. As I expected, he asked me to lie down so that he could examine my bump and make sure things were ok. I always find those encounters awkward – where do you look? It's so strange when someone is so close to you, in your personal space, poking and prodding you in all of your "personal areas".

Anyway, shortly after my examination finished, he smiled at me and said (I kid you not), "Well, your bump is pretty big! Are you sure you only have one in there?!". Before I could even gather myself together, I snorted back, "Are *you* sure you haven't got any in *there*?" and pointed to his not-very-flat stomach.

Now, my intention wasn't to body shame him – of course not! But he had body shamed *me*, and made me feel so horrendous that I just wanted to bite back. He clearly didn't like my response, so began to explain again that my bump really *was* on the large side and that maybe I should consider trying not to eat so much or going on a diet! I couldn't really process my thoughts as he started throwing medical jargon at me, talking about my BMI, and bringing up the word that probably frightens me the most when it comes to health – and that is "risk".

Pregnant or not, when you're over a certain number on the scales and come up against a health issue, someone is likely to want to relate it back to your weight. It's frustrating, but not uncommon. This isn't just something I'm assuming here; there have been several studies conducted over recent years that evidence that unconscious bias from medical professionals as regards someone's weight is more common than you think. For example, a study conducted at Wake Forest School of Medicine in the US between 2008 and 2011 rather shockingly showed that more than a third of medical school students had a bias against people who were classed as "obese", whether the students were aware of it or not.

These worrying statistics mean that many "overweight" patients will not go to their medical professional to seek care for conditions, even if they are *entirely* unrelated to their weight, as the stigma attached to their size makes them feel that the ensuing conversations are likely to be demeaning, upsetting and make them feel even worse! A shocking situation!

When I started to do some research, I soon found out that this BMI scale being used to measure the "success" of our health, was created back in the 1830s by a Belgian astronomer and mathematician called Adolphe Quetelet, who had called it the Quetelet Index at the time. Perhaps unsurprisingly for the time, had used only white, straight-identifying men to create his original scale. The female BMI chart was then created using estimations. And no other factors, such as ethnic group or body ability, were taken into consideration. Even now, the BMI scale actually differs depending on which country you live in.

As I continued to try to navigate the societal expectations around bodies via my own personal research, I came across the "body positivity movement", and suddenly felt like a whole new world had opened up to me – somewhere I felt there might finally be space for me!

BODY POSITIVITY VERSUS BODY CONFIDENCE, ETC

I would like to take a moment here to outline the difference between body positivity, body confidence, body acceptance, body neutrality and body liberation – terms that often all get accidentally rolled into one and used interchangeably.

I hope by presenting them in this way that you will gain a little more understanding of each one, and have a chance to consider which of the terms might feel most apt to you – in terms of either how you currently feel about your body, or indeed how you would ideally like to feel about it in the future – as you progress on your journey of self-love, authentic confidence and Owning It ...

Body Positivity

The body positivity movement is a social movement that was initially created to encourage acceptance, visibility and empowerment of the bodies we don't always see, including Black and ethnic minority bodies, as well as bodies of *all* sizes; the bodies that are not on billboards or the front covers of magazines. Some of the key goals of the movement are: to address the unrealistic body standards imposed through societal "norms"; to help people feel confident in the body they are in; to promote acceptance of *all* bodies, regardless of ability, race, gender or size; and to challenge how society defines and views bodies and worthiness.

The roots of this movement started in the late 1960s within the Fat Acceptance Movement. Pretty self-explanatory from the name, the Fat Acceptance Movement was about tackling fat-shaming and discrimination against those who were seen as fat, overweight or obese. The National Association to Advance Fat Acceptance (NAAFA) was then established in 1969, and continues to work to change how people talk about weight. Various other movements and groups have emerged since then, but it was when the EffYourBeautyStandards movement (created in 2012 by Tess Holiday, the first plus-size supermodel signed to a major model agency) took off on Instagram that visibility was really increased around marginalized bodies, and a more active celebration of different body types started to flourish. And this at least *started* to openly and actively challenge many of the societal norms around the "desired" body shapes and sizes that are so often promoted in the media.

Body Confidence

Also referred to as "body image", this is someone's perception of how they look physically, or how sexually attractive they feel in their own body. Body confidence is about how someone sees themselves compared to society's beauty standards.

Body Acceptance

This is the feeling of accepting your body as it is – regardless of whether you feel happy or confident with all areas of it. Body acceptance is about wholeheartedly accepting that this is your body in the current moment, and being comfortable with that.

Body Neutrality

This is about focusing on non-physical attributes that your body has and what it is capable of *doing*, rather than its appearance. Similar to body acceptance, body neutrality is about challenging the way you feel about and/or describe your body, and not centralizing its worth only on what it looks like.

Body Liberation

This is about seeking freedom from the weight of the societal standards that tend to put more value on bodies that they deem to be physically fit, healthy and beautiful. The concept of body liberation is a big middle finger to the idea that some bodies are more worthy than others, and seeks to include *all* bodies, despite what they look like or their perceived level of health.

BODY INCLUSIVITY

I'm a firm believer that, whether you're a size 6, 16, 26 or 36, you deserve to feel good about yourself – positive, confident, accepting *and* liberated. It's your birthright. (You don't need to fit within a certain size or weight limit to have the right to confidence, self-esteem and self-love.)

I think it's important to understand the difference between the various terms above though, as I've noticed that at times the body *positivity* movement (about inclusivity of marginalized bodies that have generally not been represented or visible in mainstream media) has been somewhat highjacked by voices that I think more naturally sit within the body *confidence* camp (about personal perception of your own body) – by voices (and bodies) that are *not* marginalized, voices that are mainstream, *not* invisible.

We therefore need to be sure to create space for the people who have not been represented – either positively, or at all. And we need to protect this space. So I want to be clear that what I'm talking about in this chapter, and in this book, is body confidence and body acceptance.

ACCEPTING YOURSELF

Feeling good, and confident, about your body doesn't come naturally to most. You can be a size 8, petite, blonde, blue-eyed woman and see bodies that look like yours all over the place – on billboards, in magazines and on the front of every health magazine – but that doesn't mean you automatically get a self-love switch! I think this is important to highlight, as having a negative body image definitely isn't exclusive to just those who are fat, plus size and big-boned! Actually, it's often got very little, if anything, to do with what your *actual* body looks like.

So, where do you start on the journey to loving your own body? I've learned, over time, that acceptance is often the first step. I've said it before and will say it again, as it applies to so many different aspects of life: acceptance is not about "settling" or giving up on dreams and aspirations; it's about simply consenting to the fact that this is where you are *now* – and, whether you are entirely happy with it or not, it is ok. It is perfectly ok.

In my own journey to self-love, I kind of skipped, hopped and jumped over body acceptance in my eagerness to get to the confident bit. And, while I got there in the end, there have been elements of my journey that I have had to do some serious backtracking on in order to learn to truly *accept* my body as it is. Two of the key actions that helped lead me to my current place of accepting the skin I'm in are as follows:

Appreciate the Journey Until Now

How often do we look back and really appreciate all the things that our bodies have been through in our lives? It seems to me that, unless they have had to recover from some specific big trauma like a car accident, a serious illness or whatever else, we often take them for granted, forgetting to acknowledge just how much they do for us.

I think it was when I had my children that I first started to really pay attention to just how amazing our bodies are! The whole process of new life being created within us completely fascinated me – and woke me up to all the other incredible ways that my body had served me over the years.

The fantastic thing here is that you don't have to like what your body *looks* like in order to really appreciate what it has done for you – and continues to do for you. So this is a beautiful place to start your journey to self-love: simply accepting the greatness of your body every single day as it functions for you. If you can practise this kind of daily appreciation of your body, it's already a huge step forward.

How it Feels Versus How it Looks

Another game changer for me was realizing the utmost importance of making decisions – whether what to wear, what to eat, what to do or anything else – based on how things made me *feel* (or *might* make me feel), rather than how I felt that they made me *look* (or *might* make me look)!

Exercise was a good example of this. I had never liked it. It felt like something I was bad at and would embarrass myself doing. And, quite frankly, I couldn't be bloody bothered! When I did force myself to do some though, my sole focus was always on changing how my body *looked* – mainly by making it smaller! I never focused on the benefits for my health, strength or fitness levels – and how much better I could *feel* as a result of it. Thankfully, this all changed when I started going to Zumba classes in 2015, and I realized just much I enjoyed it (I've always loved to dance). The fact that it simply made me *feel* good was far more important than how many calories it might burn or how much smaller it might make my body. And that's why I'm still Zumba-ing away to this day!

THE PRESSURE FOR PERFECTION

I've spent a lot of time in my life (and a lot of money!) trying to make myself smaller so that people who were unkind to me, body-shamed me, or who seemed to not like me because of the way I looked, would have less to say or would maybe suddenly just accept me.

But at some stage on my journey I realized that the most toxic form of body shaming wasn't the strangers making wild comments on the Internet, the friends less than half my size but who continue to complain that they are fat, or the people in the office who disguise fat jokes as banter. The most toxic form of body shaming was the things that I had been saying to myself! Such as, if only I wasn't quite so "big/fat/enormous/elephant-like" and whatever else, then people might like me!

Whether we talk about it or not, most of us feel a constant pressure to look a certain way. This has been embedded in us since we were young, without us even knowing it; we've been exposed to things like slim, pretty Disney princesses and perky, "perfect" Barbie dolls, as if these are the kind of physical images we are meant to strive for, and the kind of woman who lands her dream job, gets her prince and lives her best life! (Apparently, by the way, if a human actually had the relative measurements of Barbie, she wouldn't be able to stand, as the measurements are so off!)

An online survey conducted in 2019 by the Mental Health Foundation with global public opinion and data company YouGov, highlighted that 37% of teenagers in the UK felt sad about their bodies and 31% felt ashamed of them, sometimes affecting children as young as eight. I know that I, personally, have found it utterly exhausting trying to navigate how I feel about my body in today's image-obsessed world. It's pretty scary just how much it affects us!

So what do you do? What do you do when you just want to feel as confident as possible about the body you're in, but it feels like everyone around you is telling you, whether directly or indirectly, that you need to change it or "fix" it?

STEPS TO BODY CONFIDENCE

I have said it before, but building your confidence isn't an overnight process; it's one that takes consistent practice and nurturing. Everyone's journey to body confidence will be different, but here are some of the quick wins and more long-term changes that I made to support my journey to feeling more comfortable in my own skin.

Buy Clothes that Fit

If you need an excuse to go shopping, then here it is ...

If you're anything like me, there's a pair of old jeans (or potentially much more!) sitting in a wardrobe somewhere that you will "eventually fit into". They've been there for years now, and (sorry!) you may well never fit into them again. I'm not saying that there's no point in setting goals or hoping for change, but the thing is that every time you try on or even look at those jeans – or any other clothes that are even slightly too tight or unflattering in any other way – it's likely to be an unwelcome reminder that your body isn't as it used to be, or isn't as you'd like it to be, which means you may instantly feel bad about your body.

But the thing is: clothes are made to fit your body; your body is not made to fit your clothes! So why not simply get clothes that fit it! It is, after all, completely natural that our bodies shift in shape and size with time, so it would be better for us all if we could just accept that as normal, rather than carrying any embarrassment, guilt or shame about it.

I recently realized that if I needed a bigger size shoe, I wouldn't hesitate to get it. No guilt or shame. Just a bigger size shoe. But, unfortunately, the same feelings often don't apply to buying bigger jeans or dresses, etc! So, when buying bigger clothes (which will ultimately look better as well as being more comfortable!), try not to put such value on size. The important thing is how the clothes make us *feel* rather than what size they are!

Getting up in the morning and putting on something that fits well, is comfortable and brings you joy can make an enormous difference to how confident you feel as you set about each day.

Thank Your Body

Taking a moment to feel grateful for the things that your body does for you every day will give you a level of appreciation for it that you didn't have before. When I started doing this, I couldn't really think of anything that I was thankful for. But I soon realized that I was overthinking things (and essentially trying too hard!), so I started to simply notice things to be grateful for as they were happening.

As I type this, for example, I thank my fingers and hands for being able to type, I thank my mouth for smiling and showing the world that I am happy, I thank my body for holding me upright – as well as for having carried and birthed my beautiful children, who I can hear in the next room. Once you start being able to notice the positive things like this, you'll become aware of more and more.

Another key moment for me in learning to be more thankful for my body was after my daughter Isabella had fallen over one day at the park. She had grazed her knee pretty badly and, for weeks after, would show us her graze every day and tell us the story of when she fell over. Then, one day when she went to show us as normal, her scab had gone. The learning for me though was that she couldn't stop saying "Mummy, my knee better! My knee better! My ouch has gone!" – with the most beautiful look of amazement on her face at how it had all gotten "magically" better!

Her incredulity at the healing of her knee reminded me of just how incredible it really is that our bodies are capable of healing the way they do. I had never really stopped to thank my body for this before – after every time that I had tripped, walked into a door, stubbed my toe or whatever else.

So try it for yourself – thank your body as often as you can for all the little ways in which it supports and protects you – and allow yourself to accept just how wonderful your body truly is.

Get Naked

This one isn't easy at all and took me a long time to get my head around. Just to be clear – it's not about getting naked for, or in front of, anyone else. The task I set myself here was to look at my *own* full-length naked body in a mirror and accept it for what it was.

There's a level of vulnerability that comes with being naked that is hard to deal with even when you're on your own, never mind with anyone else. And I had always been a lights-off, keep-as-many-clothes-on-as-possible kind of girl when I was in intimate relationships. So it took me a long time to be able to bring myself to stand boldly in front of the mirror in my birthday suit.

I had so feared what I might see and how I might feel that when I finally plucked up the courage to do it, it wasn't as bad as I had expected! While the first few times felt odd and I lasted all of a few seconds, over time I got so used to seeing my body that I couldn't understand (or really even remember) what I had ever feared so much. My body was just a body. It was keeping me alive – giving me the privilege of breathing, walking and talking. So why on earth had I ever been so scared of it?

The more I made looking at my naked body in the mirror part of my daily routine, alongside some deeper "mirror work" (see page 180), the more I was able to settle into a feeling of increased ease and confidence with my body. So I encourage you to try it for yourself ... I know it's not easy. (Honestly, I do!) But it really will be worth it in the end, as you start to love your body purely for the beautiful, functioning miracle that it is, rather than placing all the unrealistic aesthetic expectations on it that we so often do.

Mirror Work

In its most simple form, mirror work is a lot like what I've just described, but without the need to get your kit off (unless you really want to!). It involves speaking positively to yourself – to open up an empowering dialogue about the physical aspects of your own body. (Yip! I totally advocate a good natter with yourself now and again!).

I first came across mirror work as a means of promoting body confidence and acceptance courtesy of wellbeing author Louise Hay, who is a strong advocate for the use of positive affirmations – ideally for at least 21 days in a row to help build a new habit (although others, such as motivation coach Lisa Nichols, suggest a minimum of 30 days).

Louise Hay believes that affirmations have the biggest impact when you say them out loud to yourself while looking in the mirror. And I have to admit that I think she is right. But I'll be honest – doing this can feel beyond awkward when you start. You can barely believe it's come to this. And you feel strange and embarrassed, despite the fact nobody else is around or even knows you're doing it!

Please trust me, however, when I say that this sense of embarrassment will soon melt away as you realize just how much the benefits of the practice outweigh the temporary discomfort. Among the many upsides are enhanced self-confidence, self-trust and, yes, self-love, too – even for me of my beautiful five-foot-two

(1.57m), plus-size body, which I had once so struggled to even look at, never mind accept and love. See the GUIDED TASK (page 191) for a 30-day Mirror Work Challenge to get you started on your own journey to increased body confidence.

SEEING YOURSELF AS WHOLE

When we look at ourselves in the mirror, especially when looking for a length of time, such as during Mirror Work, we all too often see our body as a collection of separate areas – our belly, our bum, our arms, our thighs, etc ...

Some areas we might think are ok. Some we don't pay too much attention to. Some we declare as our "problem areas". And some we avoid looking at all together. In the process, we chop ourselves up into little pieces for analysis without appreciating the gloriousness of our body in its entirety. We forget how our body works as a whole, each part with its own incredible function and purpose.

One of the best analogies I've heard for this was about flat tyres on a car. The question was put to me: if you had one flat tyre, would you be angry at the whole car? Would you be horrible and abusive to the car even though there was just one tyre that needed mending? Of course we wouldn't! Yet this is what we do to ourselves. There might well be an area here and there that we aren't entirely happy with – and that's ok; we are human after all. But just because we're not keen on that one area, doesn't mean that we should tear our entire body apart, including completely unrelated parts that we might not even mind – saying things like

"I'm soo disgusting!" – rather than just recognizing that we would, for example, like to work on toning up our stomach and our thighs.

When we begin to see ourselves as a beautiful whole, we can accept the parts of us that we may want to work on as just part of us, rather than allowing them to dominate everything. As mentioned earlier in this chapter, you don't have to be happy with everything about yourself right now, but it's good to accept and embrace that this is where you are right now – and that this is where you can now happily move forward from ...

REDEFINING BEAUTY

What do the words "beauty" and "beautiful" really mean to you?

Digging deep into what I truly thought beauty was gave me the opportunity to realize just how much diversity it can encompass. I came to see that, although I had been constantly chasing a particular goal of what I thought I needed to be in order to be "beautiful" myself, I actually saw beauty in almost everything and everyone but myself. I could see the glory and wonder in someone else's cellulite or stretch marks. I could delight in the confidence and prettiness of other women, whether super slim or plus-size. And I could generally see beauty all around. I just couldn't see it in *me!* So I decided to put pen to paper in order to redefine and get clearer on my own notion of beauty.

I realized that, to me, beauty is everywhere. It's in sunsets and colourful flowers. It's in each and every body shape and size – tall or short, big or small, slim or curvy. It's in long hair, short hair, straight hair, curly hair and no hair. It's in body hair or no body hair. It's in any colour eyes. It's in delicate dimples of cellulite. It's in dark purple stretch marks. It's in both feminine and masculine. Beauty isn't just skin deep. It's everything about a person: their compassion, their kindness, their intelligence, their humour, their humility and all the rest.

And once I realized that beauty was everywhere and that I could see it in pretty much everything, I knew that I would, eventually, be able to see it in myself, too. I just needed to believe and start taking the actions to open my eyes to the beauty in myself.

BEING GENTLE

If we wanted to show love to someone we cared about, we would be tender, gentle and considerate in the way we physically interact with them, right? Yet we often don't really consider this when it comes to ourselves.

This particularly struck me one day a while back while I was washing my hair. I suddenly became aware of the fact that I almost always tug roughly at it and just get it done as fast as I can, as if I have better things to be doing with my time! Yet if I ever went to a hairdresser who washed my hair in the manner that I washed my own, I would certainly never go back! And I might even complain about how I was treated!

So I now take my time with this (when I have the time to take). I try to wash my hair as a hairdresser would. I'm mindful of the water temperature. I massage my scalp. And I do the same with my skincare routine, taking five minutes for it both in the morning and the evening – five minutes that make me feel like I'm at a mini spa.

By implementing these simple ways of being more gentle with myself, I'm showing myself that I am worth it – valued, precious and deserving of the same respect and love that I would show someone else.

So try it for yourself. Decide on at least one thing that you're going to do every day from here on in to show your body love and respect. This is personal to your journey, but if you feel you need guidance, feel free to choose from the list below:

- Drink more water
- Implement a regular skin care routine
- Spend five minutes in front of the mirror, saying positive affirmations about your body
- Move your body! Whether it's via a kitchen disco or a gym workout (just do what makes you feel good!)
- Wear nice comfortable clothes that you feel good in
- Scroll less on your devices
- Honour both your hunger and your fullness – eat when you feel hungry and stop when you feel full; this way, you'll be respecting your body's natural processes and there should be no need to either deny yourself or over-indulge (after which we always feel terrible anyway!)

TOUCHING YOUR BODY

I'm not about to get cheeky in this section, I promise (although if you want to go down there, you totally should!). I'm bringing up the subject of self-touch as I spent a long time being unable to touch pretty much any part of my own body.

After a friend's breast cancer diagnosis a few years back, I started mentioning breast checks more on my social media platforms – as a means of promoting increased health awareness (early detection is so vital in any diagnosis, yet something that many of us wouldn't think to consider). But on recommending this to others, I realized that I hadn't really touched my own breasts before! In fact, I hadn't really touched many areas of my body, as I was afraid I wouldn't like how they felt and that it would lead me further into the negativity that I already felt.

There were two levels to this for me – one was practical (so that I could get to know my body better and have more chance of knowing if something didn't feel medically right); and the other was emotional (as I knew I needed to establish a better connection with my body if I was ever going to accept and love it more).

So I began to check my breasts regularly (and I'd strongly suggest that you do too, as it's always better safe than sorry). Touching myself in this way felt like a strange thing to do at first. But, in not very much time at all, body parts such as my breasts and stomach, which I would once have avoided touching all together, became to me just parts of my body that exist, that are there, and that are wonderful exactly as they are.

I now touch my body daily, whether in the shower or doing my regular boob checking, and I feel so strongly that we should be doing this as often as possible. Please note that all genders should check their breast tissue and all areas of their body as often as possible for any changes. If you are unsure how to check, head over to www.coppafeel.org where you will find step-by-step guidance, as well as the option to set up a free text reminder to get checking more often.

DIVERSIFYING WHAT YOU CONSUME

I'm a big fan of social media, but there's no getting away from the fact that what we consume online has a huge impact on our body image. Diversifying what you expose yourself to – your feed, movies and TV that you watch, articles that you read, etc – can really broaden your view of just how many different incredible bodies exist in the world.

There is so much greatness in opening your eyes (and your mind) to just how varied and wonderful the world is, and the many different bodies that make it up. And the more you are exposed to a range of bodies, the more you are likely to be able to love your own in the knowledge that there are so many ways to exist, that there is no one definition of beauty, and that there is beauty everywhere we choose to see it.

Owning It Top Tip

Diversify your social media feed to ensure that the content you are regularly exposed to is as reflective as possible of the many varied shapes, sizes, colours and creeds of people and movements that are out there (see Useful Resources for a useful starting point list).

ACCEPTING THAT IT'S NOT ALL REAL

It's important to know that many of the images we are seeing in the media are simply often not real. Photoshop and other picture-augmenting tools are being used every single day to manipulate the body size and shape, skin colour and texture, hair colour and style (and more) of the people we are being shown in ads, on magazine covers and sometimes even just in family holiday photos shared on Facebook! The end result is that a lot of what we are being fed as aspirational "reality" simply isn't "real" at all! It's therefore really important that we don't fall into the trap of comparing our own realities with other people's carefully curated surface displays!

On this basis, I try to seek out as many magazines, media outlets and online platforms to follow that don't use filters or heavy editing – so that I know the images I'm seeing from these sources are as real as possible and that I can accept them as at least in some way representative of reality.

You may wish to do the same, so look out for pages and hashtags that mention things like #NoFilter or #FilterFree to identify safe spaces online where the images are not altered in anyway and are a truer reflection of reality.

AVOIDING COMPARISON

The importance of avoiding comparison has been a recurring theme in this book as it applies to so many different areas of life. But here I am again, about to go on about it …

Comparing your own body to someone else's will never get you anywhere! Every single person has different DNA, so even if you ate, worked out and did exactly the same thing as someone else did, your body still wouldn't look exactly like theirs.

And anyway, why would we want it to be like someone else's when the beauty of life is that we're all so different and unique!? The key to it all is really accepting and respecting our uniqueness – in order to be able to truly embrace our own bodies for what they are, and to love the skin we're in.

Self-Reflection Questions

On Embracing Your Body & Loving the Skin You're In

- How do I currently feel about my body? And why might this be?
- Are there things that I would like to change about my body? If so, why?
- What do I tend to place more emphasis on – how I feel about things or how they're likely to make me look?
- What does being beautiful really mean to me?
- Are there particular people or things that make me feel negative about my body?
- What things about my body am I most grateful for?

GUIDED TASK
Body Gratitude

This feel-good exercise gives you the chance to feel into and write down all the things about your body that you are grateful for. Whether you are at the start of your body acceptance journey or are further down the line, it's the ideal way to give yourself a boost in confidence and self-esteem by highlighting all the wonderful things that your body does for you on an ongoing basis.

What To Do

1. Identify a part of your body that you feel grateful for and write it down as part of the gratitude statement below, completing the statement with the *reason* for your gratitude:

    "Thank you body. Thank you for my ...
    which allow(s) me to ..."

    Then, one at a time, do the same for other parts of your body that you feel grateful for.

    Examples that I have come up with in the past include:

- "Thank you body. Thank you for my eyes, which allow me to take in the wonders of the world and see my beautiful children's faces."
- "Thank you body. Thank you for my breasts, which have allowed me to nourish three children and make me feel sexy."
- "Thank you body. Thank you for my hands, which have allowed me to care for myself physically, hold my babies and write this book!"

2. Once you have written out your body gratitude statements, read them out loud to yourself. Feel free to do this several times if you wish – to help let the gratitude really sink in.

3. Return to this list of self-affirming body statements any time you realize that you're being hard on yourself and/or could do with a lift.

GUIDED TASK
30-Day Mirror Work Challenge

This challenge involves dedicating a set amount of time each day over 30 consecutive days to saying positive, present-tense, first-person affirmations to yourself while looking in the mirror.

The only rule of the challenge is that you have to stick to it *every single day* – no matter what mood you are in and no matter what has happened during the day ... Consistency of practice is key.

What Does It Involve?

There is no right or wrong time to do this each day. Many people prefer the morning as it can help to set the day up with a positive mindset, but feel free to do it any time that you're able to get a few minutes alone.

You can repeat the same affirmations every day or you can use different ones each time, based on what you feel you need for the day.

You don't have to believe what you are saying in the moment. The point of the challenge is for you to say nice things about yourself enough times so that as the weeks pass by you might just start to accept them more – and maybe even fully believe them. As such, please don't worry if it feels awkward, silly or false at first – just trust the process and keep going ...

What You Will Need

- A mirror – the bigger the better really – so that you can get used to seeing the whole of yourself; if you don't have a full-length mirror, even a pocket mirror will still do the job
- A timer of some sort – there'll be one on your phone
- Pre-written affirmations (optional) – this can make things easier when you first start if you are struggling to think of positive things to say to yourself

What To Do

1. Stand in front of your mirror fully clothed, in your underwear or butt naked! However you want, but, ideally, somewhere quiet, where you will not be disturbed (especially if you're naked!)

2. Decide what positive statements you would like to hear today, and feel free to write them down on a piece of paper or in a notebook if desired. Between one and three statements is enough.

Here are some examples:

- I love my body and myself
- I look great today
- My body does so many incredible things for me
- This body deserves love and respect
- My worth is not defined by my size
- I am allowed to take up space
- I accept my body exactly as it is in this moment
- I am beautiful
- I am safe
- I am loved

3. Set a timer for the allocated length of time depending on which day of your 30-day challenge you are on:

- Days 1–7: 1 minute
- Days 8–14: 2 minutes
- Days 15–21: 4 minutes
- Days 22–30: 5 minutes

4. Start saying your chosen affirmation(s) out loud until the time finishes.

And there you have it! You have now taken a small but worthwhile step on your journey to increased confidence, liberation and joy.

Chapter 6

Successfully Navigating the Sea of Social Media

Are you ancient enough (like me!) to remember Myspace? For those too young to know, it was basically Facebook and Instagram's much older cousin who, at one point, was the coolest member of the family, and totally the person you wanted to be around! You couldn't wait until they walked in at a family function, because you knew that it would then be fun! This was until you got older, when you realized that they were actually pretty weird! And now nobody ever mentions them! I often find myself wondering at what point Instagram will become similarly archaic and we will be referring to the good old days of double-tapping and how weird it was to watch hours of stories.

As well as Myspace, there were the delights of BEBO and Profilepic (if you know, you know). And if you want to throw it right back, there was the wonder of MSN Messenger. The holy grail of Internet chat at the time. The place you would get kicked off when your Mum needed to use the house phone. And the place you logged on and off from repeatedly, in the hope that your crush would notice the notification that you were online, too – in the days of indirect declarations of love by putting up your favourite song lyric as your online name!

So, while I have used the Internet for the best part of almost 20 years (WTF!), I never *planned* to play my life out on it. I mean, goals for me when I was a child involved wanting to be a backing dancer in MTV music videos or a school teacher (I know, I didn't exactly have a theme in mind and I wasn't very consistent, but I was only 12 – give a girl a break!).

As I mentioned at the start of the book, when I first started on Instagram back in 2014, it was with a weight loss account, which I used as both a food diary and a place to get motivation for the 94th diet that I was hoping to finally stick to! Fast forward seven years and here I am, sharing my whole flippin' life on the Internet for whoever clicks, follows or fancies a gander. It's pretty obvious that it's not a weight loss account anymore; my thick thighs can also attest to that! It's now more of a safe space where I share the realities of being a mother, a wife and navigating the world in a plus-size body confidently (at last!). Being "The Fat Funny One" (alongside the diversity and inclusion work that I do in the world of recruitment) certainly isn't a role that I ever imagined for myself, but it is one that I am totally in love with … most of the time at least.

As with all jobs, there are highs and lows. Some days you're buzzing and can't wait to see all your colleagues for a catch-up, you're happy to be working on an exciting project, or you're glad to succeed in a task that has made you remember why you love it. But there are also days when you have to check your bank balance to remind yourself why you need to haul your ass out of bed and do what you do for eight hours a day, while you drown your sorrows in cheap coffee and send passive aggressive emails.

I often get asked what the lows are about sharing so much of my life online and allowing everyone to have "access" to me and my life. And my answer is always that it leaves me open to everyone giving me their opinion of me, whether I like it or not!

I talked earlier about the negativity that I used to receive (and still do) about my appearance. To some degree, I guess, I expected some comments on this kind of thing, as it's what people instantly see online when they come across you. They don't know much about you, so the majority of their comments (whether negative or positive) will tend to be around what you look like. People's obsession with aesthetics is so engrained that they will often come by to comment on that alone – with no other information, knowledge or discussion. I guess it's no different from people making snap judgements and assumptions about others as they walk past them on the street, except that the platform for the comments is so much more public!

However, what *did* surprise me were the assumptions, questions, digs and insults around my character and who "The Fat Funny One" really is, as a person. It's one thing calling me fat and commenting on my body, but it's another thing questioning the safety of my children, whether or not I'm a good mother and basically more or less every decision that I make for myself or family. Call me naïve, but that surprised me!

Social media has become such a huge part of our everyday lives that we often forget how much control we actually have over what we choose to consume online. The reality is that while we are unable to control other people's opinions, how they live, what they say, or even how triggering we may find something, we *are* able to control what we consume, how much we consume, when we consume it, or whether we consume at all. Let me give you an analogy – it's food related (obviously).

WHAT'S ON YOUR SOCIAL MEDIA PLATE?

If social media was a buffet and your mind was the plate, you would fill it with all the things you love, right? (Totally spending a lot of time at the dessert section.) You wouldn't waste space on your plate with things that you hate! (That wasn't meant to rhyme, but I'm a lyrical G!) Moving on, taking up valuable plate space with things you don't even like would be ridiculous, right? You would simply walk past anything that doesn't take your fancy, ignoring it. I mean, you *might* have a little look, poke it with your spoon, read the little menu card or even give it a sniff. But if it's something that you know you won't like the taste of, or will have a bad effect on you, you'd just pass on by and spend your time filling up your "plate" with all the things that bring your taste buds joy!

This is how we should manage our social media. Your mind is your plate – a valuable, precious plate that you only have one of. So it's best to treat it with the utmost caution, like you would your Nana's best china. And it's best *not* to pile it high with things that you don't even want and then run the risk of dropping it due to the weight!

Now, Lord knows, I love me a buffet and I love me some social media, so it has been a real journey for me getting a grip on what I really want on my social media plate – not only how good it will taste for me but how it will serve me in the long run. I realized after a while after discovering this social media plate approach that it wasn't just some exercise that would make me feel a little bit better – it was a true act of self-love that started to transform how I felt about myself (and others) as soon as I started putting it into action.

Before I became aware of managing what, and how much, was on my plate, I used to pile it all on – both in the figurative sense of social media and at the actual buffet! I followed everyone who seemed worth following – sometimes just because everyone else did, as I didn't want to be the one person who wasn't "in" on something. I suffered with major FOMO (fear of missing out) – I always wanted to know what was going on and when. And I became unhealthily invested in other people's lives – from what they were wearing, where they were going on holiday, and, God help me, whether there was a swipe-up link to a cushion that they had just bought! While all these kinds of things are almost the purpose of social media, I found that my balance wasn't a healthy one. My plate was filled with pages and people that constantly made me feel "not good enough". Whether it was because of their incredible bodies, on-trend outfits or perfectly pleasing boho-chic living rooms, everything that I was looking at was making me feel like I just wasn't part of the cool gang and that maybe there was something wrong with me!

ADDICTED TO SCROLLING

I'm going to throw some stats at you now, which are a little bit scary but so eye-opening. There are two billion of us across the world (yes, two *billion!*) who use social media on a daily basis. And when Harvard University did a study (in 2021) around how addictive social media could be – both physically and psychologically – it, rather worryingly, showed that self-disclosure (sharing personal information) online can fire up the same part of the brain that is activated when taking addictive substances! I told you it was scary! But in a way I'm not surprised. There are so many things that happen without us even knowing that keep us constantly scrolling. It's a little bit like Dory in *Finding Nemo* – social media platforms are singing to our subconscious, "Just keep swimming (scrolling!)".

We are conditioned throughout so much of our lives to live in a place of lack – and what I mean by that is that we constantly feel as if we need more. We are rarely fulfilled by what we have and, whether we recognize it or not, we tend to search for that "more" outside of ourselves, including on the endless cycle of social media that we have at our fingertips 24/7 these days. When not managed well, our constant scrolling can therefore be like regularly comfort eating huge piles of sweets on an empty stomach – something that seems like a great idea at the time but ends up making you feel sick afterward, as well as hungry again shortly after!

I often used to find myself scrolling through people's online lives and feeling frustrated for not being invited to events hosted by people I didn't even know, being jealous of opportunities that other people had worked hard for and, more often than any of those, being upset and angry that my physical appearance didn't match those who were having the events, getting the opportunities and living the life that I wanted but felt that I would never obtain.

But here's the thing: the problem wasn't that I couldn't obtain these things that I was looking at and longing for – the problem was that the things I was chasing after in my mind didn't actually exist in the real world! From the perfect pictures of happy families with well-behaved children on Facebook and the sculpted bodies without a touch of cellulite on Instagram to the Pinterest-worthy interiors and the happy couples vlogging their way around the most tropical paradise on YouTube, all of what I was consuming seemed so "perfect" that it was making me feel bad about myself and my own messy life in comparison – affirming what I already felt at the time, which was that I was just wasn't good enough to get any of the wonderful things that all these *other* people had! What I didn't realize at the time, however, is that I was comparing the *reality* of my life to the glossy *image* of perfection that others were presenting to the world; not their own messy reality, that was undoubtedly just beneath the surface!

INSTAGRAM VERSUS REALITY

Nowadays when I'm online, I try and paint a really honest picture of what my life is like. Have I always done that? Of course not, because, like everyone else, I was taught to always put my best face forward, show the world the lovely, well put-together areas of my life; *not* the corner of the room where I've stashed all the crap or the bribes I've just given to my children after screaming "Just keep still!!" at the top of my lungs. Social media is all about sharing accomplishments, not failures: landing your dream job; not when the business you started didn't go so well and you had to close up shop. Sharing your exciting pregnancy announcements; not bringing everyone down by sharing your losses. Sharing your amazing holidays and new cars; not your scarily large credit card bills!

It has become the norm to share the goodness, the positives and the wonders of life – and, don't get me wrong, that's always a wonderful thing to do! But if that's the *only* side of things that we share, we can easily lose our sense of what real life can be like – with its fair share of hardship, heartbreak, loss, loneliness and more. If we get used to only the glossy, positive side of things being presented on social media, we can easily get stuck in a place of pretence – where we feel that we have to constantly try to make sure that we are *perceived* as being successful and happy (whether or not we are!) – and this is unbelievably exhausting!

This is no-one's fault. It happened long before we could share information instantly with thousands of people all over the world. It also happens among family circles and friendship groups *offline*. Social media (with its filters and photoshop perfection) has just exacerbated it, making it the absolute norm – so much so that we can lose sight of the simple fact that life is often beautifully chaotic, messy (and sometimes covered in cellulite)!

When Apple introduced the option to have a regular report of your screen time on your device (insert big sarcastic "thanks" here), I was genuinely horrified by the length of time that I spent online, and quite quickly noticed that my screen time correlated with how I was feeling in my "real" life. If I was online more, it was generally because I was trying to escape or disconnect from something in my life that was making me feel "less than";

whereas when I was feeling fulfilled with everyday life and enjoying myself, my screen time was at a minimum.

I once came across a quote that suggested being with someone who, when you are together, makes you forget to look at your phone. But the truth is that we don't need someone *else* to be able to live a life where we forget to check our phone, or decide that we don't want to check it so much; we can take action toward this way of life for ourselves.

I've done this a lot over the past number of years, so I'd like to share with you some of the best ways I've found to help me reach for my phone less, get more present in the "real "world and live a life where I feel fulfilled enough without the need to go online searching ...

HAVE A SOCIAL MEDIA BREAK

I first joined Facebook in 2007 (when poking each other and sending sheep was totally a thing!) – and there has been very little that I haven't shared since then! Social media is, to my mind, a brilliant way to connect with friends and family, and give information out to loads of people in one hit, such as birth announcements or what you had for dinner (I have certainly seen some dodgy looking dinners in my time!). But I find it pretty scary that although I've been online for over a decade now, it's only in the last couple of years that I've been actively having breaks from it.

When first trying to work out the sections that I wanted for my "social media plate" in 2015, I realized that I needed to come offline completely for a bit in order to reset the unhealthy habits I had fallen into (my "addiction" if you like). So I deleted the social media apps off my phone (although I didn't remove my accounts), and I really cannot recommend doing this enough! A spa day is a beautiful act of self-care, but having a break from social media is hands-down better for me (and this is coming from someone who would do anything for a massage and a fluffy white robe!).

I'm not going to lie – the first time I did it, I struggled! Despite me knowing that going offline was the break that my mind needed to try to get back on a more even mental health kilter, I found it really hard. I had just gotten so scarily used to constantly having my phone in my hand and having a quick "pop" on whenever I wanted (only to find myself watching my 65th video of parking fails seven hours later) that I felt at sea without it! Social media had become engrained into almost every aspect of my life (and it still is!).

Dedicated time offline, however, really gave my mind a chance to breathe and to process. It gave me the opportunity to really be present in my own circumstances and life without looking at anything through a filter. At first it was strange, and I couldn't really remember how we ever coped without our smart phones and being 24/7 "connected".

But now when I have my breaks (I'm actually having one as I write this book), it feels incredible. It gives me a chance to recharge, to reground myself and to think into what I want from my social media consumption and content creation when I go back online. The biggest benefit, however, of taking a break is to throw yourself fully back into "real life", as it's so easy to forget what that is in a world of filtered selfies and perfectly propped cushions.

Owning It Top Tip

Book in "official" annual leave from your social media, just like you would for time off work. It might initially seem a bit OTT to schedule it in, but I have felt so much more committed to my social media breaks since I started this – happy to have the breaks to look forward to. So get your calendar out and get booking in your time to disconnect.

TUNE INTO YOUR VALIDATION STATION

The desire to feel validated, accepted and like you belong somewhere is a feeling that none of us can escape from. It's human nature and is what affirms our self-esteem. It is something that we crave but that burns super-hot, super-fast and doesn't last long when it comes from external sources. I sometimes picture validation a bit like a gas station – a validation station if you like, with all these little pumps that we can choose from in order to fill ourselves up and keep ourselves going.

The social media pump can be very appealing – with the best price fuel, the shortest queue and the most exciting offers! But is it really the best fuel option for you?! The likes, comments, shares and engagement from anyone anywhere can be a lot to deal with – whether it's your Aunty from across the pond who always comments on how you look or thousands of followers giving you minute-by-minute feedback on how you look/what you say/what you do. And if your self-esteem relies largely (or maybe even solely) on input from other people, it can be a dangerous game to play – and one that I used to play consistently.

So stuck was I in a fragile loop of feeling validated and worthy when I was complimented or praised, that it meant I was also tormented and tortured when I was criticized or ignored. Both the positive *and* the negative online interaction held so much control over me that I needed to take the power back.

Figuring out the ways that you can feel validated in *yourself*, without any *external* influence is one of the best things you can do for yourself; I'm aware that I've identified a lot of "best things" that you can do for yourself in this book, but this really is one of them! Feeling worthy in your own right puts you back in the driver's seat of your own self-esteem, giving you control over what you allow to affect you, or not!

If you had asked me what validation "pumps" I frequently tuned into a few years ago, social media would definitely have been right up there, closely followed by the acceptance and approval of other people, my relationship status and how much money I had in the bank! Notably all *external* sources of fuel!

Learning to manage my feelings around the impact that social media was having on me (that it was often leaving me depleted rather than re-fuelled!) was one of the best ways to start my journey of *self*-validation. Self-validation is about being your own cheerleader – encouraging yourself from the inside out, being comfortable with your successes and never viewing "failing" as failure, but instead as learning. It is about giving yourself space to feel however it is you feel and laying down boundaries, both in real life and in your online space.

One of the main ways that you can do this for yourself is to ensure that the space you create for yourself online is one that *adds* to your already overflowing cup of fulfilment and worthiness, rather than being the central thing that quenches the thirst of your validation-seeking.

One of the best things I ever did for myself was start curating my feed – to give myself an online space that felt safe, diverse and inspiring – so I hope that the tips in the pages that follow will help you to make a similar kind of significant change.

CURATE YOUR FEED

The act of mindfully curating your social media feed is the practical extension of metaphorically managing your social media plate. The idea here is to really evaluate everything that you're consuming, why you're consuming it, and if it's something that you want to continue seeing in your life.

It can feel difficult to make decisions about feeds to cut out while scrolling through your list of follows, as you can feel like "unfollowing" is doing something mean. But it's not; it's simply a way of protecting your own space, which should always be the priority.

One of the things I did while offline was grabbed a notebook and pen, and wrote down the things, people, themes, topics, brands and anything else that inspired me, encouraged me, made me laugh and bought me joy. Then, when I was back online, I went through everyone and everything that I followed and if they didn't fit into one of the categories that I had written down (or another life-affirming one that I hadn't thought of), then I unfollowed or muted them.

Part of my feed curation process has also involved making sure that I don't just follow people who all have the same views as me, look similar to me, are one particular body type or are at the same point as me in their self-development journey, because I don't want my social media to become an echo chamber of things that I'm already thinking and feeling.

This isn't a game of tokenism. Instead, ensuring a diverse social media feed is about opening your mind to learning new things, seeing other lifestyles and cultures, having at least a little daily insight into the beautifully diverse world in which we live and learning to live with more compassion and empathy for those around us.

As a result of adopting this outlook, I now follow so many incredible people, families, brands, charities and educational pages that I wouldn't have naturally looked at before. And I am learning so much from them – and feeling grateful to live in a world where there are so many diverse, amazing people doing so many wonderful things.

Here are a few tips for successfully curating your feed (see also the GUIDED TASK on page 215):

- **Ask for recommendations.** Friends and family will often be only too happy to recommend new inspiring pages or people that might fit into the social media categories that you would now like to focus on – so don't be afraid to ask.

- **"Pages like this."** On most social media platforms, similar pages to the ones that you already follow are likely to be recommended to you, so look out for these. On Instagram, for example, you can click the small down arrow on the right-hand side of someone's profile to see pages similar to the one that you're already on.

- **Search and follow hashtags.** This can be done on almost all social media platforms and is a great way of finding topics or causes that you would like to follow or become more involved in. I have often searched for things like #BodyConfidence and, more specifically, I once looked for #Mumsofthree when I had just had my third child and wanted to see other parents with the same! You can also follow hashtags so that if other similar content comes up using that hashtag, you will be notified and can have a look!

- **Follow pages about wider topics and causes.** Your timeline doesn't just have to be people! I follow a lot of food pages, for example (I'm not ashamed to admit it). And I also follow some great interior pages and empowerment pages. As well as sharing a lot of inspiring content of their own, such pages often then share other interesting pages or people to follow, too.

- **Tap into joy.** Your social media feed should be a place of joy for you, so don't think it has to be a constant source of life-changing inspiration. It can also simply be a place for you to have a laugh, watch funny videos or get inspiration for decorating your hallway!

SHARING ISN'T ALWAYS CARING

I'm a bonafide oversharer. I always have been. And nine times out of ten I've shared the wrong thing with the wrong person. I always had this sense that if I shared openly – both online and offline – maybe people would trust me, see my vulnerability and, dare I say it, even empathize with me and want to "play nice".

But what I've learned over the years is that it's ok to keep some things to, and for, yourself. There's a beauty in having some things that are just for *you* to know, enjoy, think about and care about. Don't get me wrong – sharing is, of course, on the whole, a good thing! But opening yourself up *all* the time can leave you exposed and potentially vulnerable, giving others opportunities that they wouldn't otherwise have to affect you in negative ways. There may, therefore, be certain areas of your life that it would be best to keep either private or limited to your inner circle, rather than sharing them publicly for all to know and comment on.

What I share online tends to change over time, and I used to beat myself up about this, putting it down to me being inconsistent. But I realized after a while that me changing what I shared actually wasn't inconsistency at all, but was, instead, me showing myself the love and respect that I deserve by trusting my gut instinct not to share certain things at certain times. Limiting what I shared, or holding certain things back, didn't make me inconsistent, fake or inauthentic; it simply protected me in areas where I was possibly more sensitive and/or vulnerable to the opinions of others, and that I might therefore find it difficult to recover from (vulnerability hangovers are totally real!).

Holding some things back isn't just about keeping things private; it's also about reinforcing the idea to yourself and your subconscious that you don't need the validation of *others* to affirm the goodness of any situation! It is great and you are great – and that doesn't change just because you're the only person who knows about it!

The best example I can give of this is getting the opportunity to write this book. Lord knows that when I got my book deal, I wanted to tell anyone and everyone. I wanted to shout it from the rooftops! I wanted to make it *known*! But when I started to reflect on *why* I wanted to share my news so much, I realized that I was seeking some sort of validation, as well as wanting to share my joy and excitement of course! I wanted to hear people tell me, "*Of course* you got a book deal – because you're amazing!". I wanted them to be surprised and delighted. I wanted them to praise me, celebrate with me and tell me lots of good things to help cover the self-doubt that was creeping in on my part. But I chose not to tell a soul – to keep it as my own special secret. And even as I write this sentence (toward the end of the book now!) – the best part of a year since the idea was first discussed – still barely anyone knows about it. And that doesn't take away even one bit from the incredible opportunity that it represents for me, the wonderfulness of it in my mind, and the fact that I really am writing a bloody book! It's still an incredible thing for me, I'm still incredible, and the world keeps moving.

So do think carefully the next time that you go to share "exciting news" – and if you realize that the main motivation for sharing feels like a desire for validation, maybe rethink your decision to share the news at all.

FIND YOUR TRIBE

There are masses of communities in pockets of the Internet where you can find incredible people with whom you might discover a sense of belonging. When I got pregnant with Sophia all those years ago, for example, I downloaded a baby bump app and met lots of fabulous women who were all on the same journey as me. So much so that, almost a decade later, many of them are still my close friends – one of whom I was a bridesmaid for, two of whom were at my wedding, and countless others of whom I have met up with on occasions over the years.

So, despite the negativity that can often be discussed when talking about the overwhelm of social media, there is also this beautiful side that encourages connection, community, support and empowerment – and I am totally up for all of this.

Don't be afraid to get to know others online. Seek out people and/or groups who will encourage you, lift you up and support you – and to whom you can offer the same level of support. Different social media platforms have different ways of going about this but, whatever the method, it generally feels just so nurturing and life-affirming when you find your "tribe", i.e. people who "just get you" and therefore make you feel less alone in the world.

THIS IS ME – TAKE IT OR LEAVE IT

I took a vow years ago that I wouldn't edit any photos before posting them online, and I've followed through on that vow. I take snaps and record vlogs with whatever mess happens to be in the background (and with whatever mess I happen to be in at the time!) as this represents the beautiful but messy reality of my life!

I don't believe in editing out the "bad" because I don't want to distort my life to fit what anyone else might think it "should" look like – whether that's what my body should look like, how I should behave, what my house should look like or what I should put out to the world. I don't believe that there is such a thing as a "perfect picture" – and that makes whatever I post totally ok with me.

I recommit to myself every day that, "This is me – take it or leave it." Affirming every day that I am comfortable with who I am, as I am, and that I know myself better than anyone can isn't easy, but my goodness is it worth it once you get the hang of it!

Social media isn't going anywhere. Whether we like it or loathe it, it's an integral part of our lives these days (often our *daily* lives). But it isn't something that needs to be feared or shied away from – somewhere that we need to project what we *could* have, *should* have or *would like to* have.

It is, instead, a place where we can choose, if desired, to be totally, authentically "us", because if more of us were willing to share the messy, chaotic and challenging parts of our lives, then slowly but surely we might just start breaking down the walls of perfection that are boxing most of us in – and preventing us from experiencing the sense of confidence, joy and freedom that we all deserve!

You have the right to be totally *you* as you navigate the stormy sea that makes up today's social media landscape, whether you share *with* others or just consume the content *of* others.

You deserve to have an online space that makes you feel good, lifts your spirits, makes you laugh and ultimately brings you joy. If you have a space where you feel safe, free and fulfilled, the more you'll start to Own your life with the help of the insights in this book.

Self-Reflection Questions

On Successfully Navigating the Sea of Social Media

- What are the current categories on my social media plate?
- Could this plate do with being rebalanced? And if so, how?
- How can I curate my social media feed to Own It more?
- What are the pumps at my validation station?
- What ways can I validate myself more, rather than seeking external validation?
- What can I gain from social media?
- What can I learn from diversifying my feed?

GUIDED TASK
Curate Your Social Media Plate

This, the final task of the book, requires you to think about all the categories of things that you would like to fill your social media plate (and therefore your mind) with – so that your daily online exposure is as uplifting and empowering as you want or need it to be. For me, this includes things like food pages, parenting advice, body-positive role models, social causes and comedy. But what will your plate look like?

What To Do

1. Make a list of all the categories of things that you would ideally like to see on your social media feed.

2. Draw a circle that represents a plate and complete it as you would do a pie chart, so that each of your categories looks like a "piece of pie" on your plate. The idea is that you can vary the size of the different pieces of pie depending on how much of your "plate" you would like each category to take up.

3. Don't worry if you need to redraw your circle a few times to get a balance that you feel happy with.

There's no right or wrong here; it's all about what works and feels best for you.

4. Now go through your social media platforms and look at who you are following. If they don't sit within the categories that you have put on your plate, begin muting or unfollowing them so that your "plate" ends up filled only with all the things that you love and can learn and benefit from!

Hey presto, you've now started to really Own your social media feed, and you're therefore one step closer to Owning It more broadly in life, too!

The Golden Nugget of Owning It

This chapter is dedicated to my beautiful friend Emma,

who taught me one of the most important life lessons to date.

Over the last few years, as my social media platforms have grown, I've been invited onto all sorts of podcasts, panels and interviews – normally to discuss the type of things that I have covered in this book. I have loved every single one and, no matter how many come up, I am filled with pure excitement – as well as complete shock! – to be invited in the first place. Especially considering that what I've been invited to talk about is self-love!

Now, I know that this is one of the main topics that I'm known for these days – and indeed that I'm writing this whole book about! – but at times it really does feel strange to me, as I still remember the me from *before* I discovered self-love. The woman who would hide in her car in the office car park because she was too afraid to face another day of constant bullying, isolation and shame. The woman who begged her cheating boyfriend to stay because a cheating boyfriend was better than no boyfriend at all! The woman who obsessed over counting calories and spent week after week attending slimming clubs that made her feel like a failure. The woman whose happiness was dictated by how many people "liked" her. The woman who relied on a small square box on the bathroom floor to let her know not only how much she weighed, but also how much she was worth! The woman who cried at her reflection in the mirror, and drank way too many VK blues in her local nightclub of a Saturday night so that she would have the confidence to dance. The woman who faked it till she made it.

That woman is a world away from where I am now. But that woman was me. And maybe that woman is you now?

All the things that I have written about in the pages of this book have played an integral part in me becoming the version of me that I am today. So it's my most sincere hope that these same insights, reflections and practical suggestions will help you on your journey to a more authentic, confident version of you, too.

The saying "Everything happens for a reason" has got to be one of the most overused (and irritating) around. Yet, annoyingly, it's also kind of true, as its main message is that if you hadn't been through everything you have, you wouldn't be the person you are today! And that really does apply to my situation! I mean, in some ways I like to naively think that I could have happily skipped a massive chunk of the drama in my earlier life and just learned the same lessons some other way, but that's just not how life tends to unfold.

When interviewers are wrapping up sessions with me, I've noticed that, no matter whether the subject is motherhood, body confidence or cake (probably the only topic I'm 100 per cent an expert on), their final question often ends up being something along the lines of: "So what is the *best* piece of advice that you would give on this topic?"

The pressure's then on for me to give a "golden nugget" answer – one piece of succinct, sound, impactful advice that has the power to change someone's life forever – and allow them to really "Own It".

I've always felt that I didn't know what to say in response to this, which led to me dreading coming to the end of interviews! Despite knowing the question was coming, in true "Jess" style, my brain would go into overdrive trying to work out for the umpteenth time which nugget, from everything I had just said, would be the most profound, the most life-changing, the most everything!

The truth was that I didn't know! I didn't ever feel able to identify *just one thing*. As I mentioned right near the start of the book, in my experience, it tends to be lots of *little* things that ultimately bring about change – lots of small, consistent decisions and actions that gradually boost your confidence, allow you to love yourself more and encourage you to embrace your body.

But while there's no denying that this is, to some extent, true, a text exchange, out of the blue, with my beautiful friend Emma got me as close to the "golden nugget" answer as I think I'm ever likely to get ...

EMMA AND HER "GOLDEN NUGGET"

Emma was my friend from high school, one of the few people from that stage of my life with whom I continued a friendship into adulthood. Ever since I remember, she exuded a confidence that I could only ever dream of – one that I often tried (and failed) to channel! She was the biggest Beyoncé fan and was our real-life Sasha Fierce. Nothing seemed to phase her. She had a self-assured way about her that you rarely saw in girls in their teens and twenties. While most of us were endlessly obsessing about what others thought of us – and wouldn't dare do anything that might jeopardize our (pretty insignificant) reputations among our peers – Emma was fearless!

She was so beautiful, with the most incredible smile. She was someone who people were just drawn to and, even though she had everything I wanted and was the kind of person I wanted to be, I never envied her. I just wanted to be *around* her because I felt that even by having a friend *like* her, I must be pretty damn cool myself!

Fast forward to a decade after school. Emma hadn't changed (thank God). She still exuded that same light-up-the-room confidence that you just wished you could bottle up and drink when you needed it the most. And that light of hers continued to shine even when she was diagnosed with breast cancer at the tender age of 26.

The next few years brought Emma on quite some journey – but that's a story that only she could tell.

I can only share what it was like witnessing it from a distance, as her friend. Because we knew her so well, we were pretty confident that if anyone was going to kick cancer in the ass, it was going to be our Queen Bee. I mean, in the school talent show, when everyone had hurried to grab friends to recreate all the '90s girl groups (I was in the Spice Girls obvs!), Emma was the only girl in the whole school who went solo – and danced to Beyoncé's *Baby Boy*. Like I said, she was fearless. So there was no doubt in our minds that, with that kind of sass from such an early age, Emma would be in remission in no time.

But things didn't go as we had hoped. In the summer of 2018, before she had even turned 29, Emma was told by the doctors that there was nothing else they could do for her.

In September 2018, Emma had one of the best parties ever. It was her 29th birthday and she had just got engaged, so we were all there to celebrate. In true Emma style, she looked a million bucks, and the party was *epic*. I remember spending parts of the evening just watching her – watching her talk to her family and friends, watching her light up the room as she always did, and watching her absolutely smash up the dance floor to a Beyoncé number.

She was doing exactly what she did best – being the life and soul of the party! But I also remember that, as I watched my amazing friend, I could really see for the first time, just how very poorly she was. Yet, for some reason, I was still completely convinced that she would be ok. Little did I realize that it would, in fact, be the last time I ever saw her.

Shortly after the party, things took a turn for the worse, and Emma got even more sick. On September 25 at 08:04, I received a message from her telling me that she was going to die.

At 29, this is *not* the kind of message you expect to get from a friend – never mind one who is three months younger than you and who you have been partying with only a week or so before.

I didn't know what to say: how do I respond to that? What words could I possibly utter that would make this any better?

Emma was so thoughtful that, even in this text message to me, she was apologizing for having to give me the news and asking if I was ok! This was the type of person she was. So, I took a deep breath and I did what I felt was right. I didn't let her know how much I was hurting, or that I was struggling to breathe through the tears that wouldn't stop. I made a joke.

Emma used to tease me because I totally had a crush on her Dad when we were at school (I really hope he or her Mum aren't reading this – awkward!). So I told her in my reply to be as blunt as she wanted or needed to be, not to worry about anyone else right now, and particularly not to worry about her family as I would totally look out for them, especially her Dad *wink emoji*.

She laughed (in text), and in her final message to me, she gave me a piece of advice that completely changed my life.

She told me she loved me, talked about our friendship and then signed off her message, "Keep doing you girl, keep doing YOU".

Emma had always been great with advice and encouragement, even during the times when she was so sick. Something that she used to say during her illness was how frustrated she felt that she was running out of time because there were so many things that she still wanted to do. Time, she would say, is the gift we all take for granted.

This, along with her "Keep doing YOU" message, lit a fire in my belly. Her words made me want to hold onto every single minute for just a little bit longer, and to finally really embrace being the only person I know how to be: me!

In the years leading up to this, I had I bought every self-help book (ironic, I know), listened to every podcast and followed every motivational person I could think of. I had worked hard at unlearning everything that "society" had taught me and at trying to become the best version of myself that I could be. But in this one simple text exchange, Emma had managed to give me the "golden nugget" answer that I had been searching for.

"Keep doing YOU," she had said.

And that's it – the answer to how absolutely *any* of us can really get the best out of life.

Three little words that sound so simple but can feel so hard at times.

So now if I were to be asked the interview question: what would my *best* piece of advice be? I'd agree with Emma, of course, by simply saying "Keep doing YOU". But I'd probably also add "Be more Emma"!

Own who the hell who you are – fearlessly and beautifully. Kick ass, wear what you want, paint your nails bright colours, be seen, be heard and dance like no-one is watching. To be fair, they normally aren't; but if they are, twerk harder!

Do whatever in the world it is that you want to do, because there is nothing in this life stopping you from becoming the person that you want to be, are capable of being and absolutely deserve to be.

At any single moment, you have the power to change your life – and to Own It 100 per cent.

Owning It Top Tip

"Be More Emma" by dancing – as often as you can! Like no-one's watching! This has to be one of the most liberating things I have learned to do! Not only does moving your body help with both physical and mental health, but it feels bloody good too!

So, whether you're on your own or with others – find a song that you love (Beyoncé is always a win for me!), turn the volume up high and let loose!

FINAL REFLECTIONS

I hope that the stories, insights and suggestions in this book have resonated with you; that you maybe now feel a little less alone, and that you have some practical tools and tricks up your sleeve on how to begin your journey to a life of more self-confidence, self-love and all-round self-fulfilment.

If I'm lucky, I might have lit a fire in your belly, like my wonderful friend Emma did for me – a fire that drives you to want to get the most out of every moment, and to know that you deserve this.

I'm so excited for you – for the journey you are about to go on, the liberation you are going to feel, and all of the joy you will create in your life. What is going to happen from here on out is going to be so great, and you deserve every single moment of the greatness that will start to unfold.

FIVE KEY WAYS TO START OWNING IT

I'd like to round things off by sharing five final steps that I've come to realize we all need to do in order to truly "Own It". So here it is – my final offering to you, my friends:

1. Do "You"
2. Start with the end in mind
3. Ask, will it matter down the line?
4. Be accountable
5. Take the first step

Do "You"

As my friend Emma said in her last ever text message to me (see page 222); "Keep doing YOU." I had spent almost all of my adult life trying to be someone else. Someone smaller, someone quieter, someone more sassy, someone prettier ... The list of the things that I tried to change is endless. But I now realize that every time I criticized myself, every time I wished I was something different, every excuse I created why I wasn't good enough/clever enough (or whatever else) to do something and every time I didn't seize an opportunity to simply be more "me", I was taking advantage of the *privilege* of time. Time isn't guaranteed; we have no control over it, yet the one thing that we *do* have control over (but that we allow ourselves to feel as if we don't) is how we feel about *ourselves* and how we treat *ourselves* – which, ironically, would change how we choose to spend our time!

When we look back over our lives one day, if we have the privilege to be able to reflect in our final moments, will all of the little things that we worry about and that we let hold us back in life really matter? The numbers on the little itchy labels stitched into our clothes? Our untameable hair? The amount of cellulite that beautifully ripples across our bodies? The scars and stretch marks that evidence the journey our bodies have been on? The people who never texted us back? The opinions of other people – some of whom we don't speak to, like or even know! Will any of those things matter? If not, then why not try to stop them from limiting our lives *now* by learning to accept and embrace them as just part of the fabric of life – so that we can start being more unapologetically ourselves. None of us are perfect – and that's ok. Our gift is that we are each the unique person that we are – in heart and mind as well as in body – so let's savour and celebrate that!

Start with the End in Mind

A few years ago, one of my best friends sent me a book as a surprise, with just a simple note to say it was brilliant. I checked out the cover and it didn't really seem my vibe at the time so I put it away and didn't pick it up again until a few years later – shortly after Emma had passed away.

And my goodness, was it at the exact point I needed it most! It has to be one of the best books I have ever read: Steven Covey's famous bestseller *The 7 Habits of Highly Effective People* (Free Press, 1989). As soon as the book kicks off, Steven talks about "starting with the end in mind". He basically discusses what you would want to hear from certain people at your funeral. I remember reading it and it feeling too raw, too soon and too strange to be discussing funerals when Emma's death felt so fresh. Yet I was drawn in and felt compelled to read the rest.

I thought about the funerals that I had recently attended, the love they were filled with and the incredible words that people had spoken about the amazing people I had been lucky enough to know. I never heard anyone mention what any of these people had looked like, what size of clothes they wore, what their hair looked like, how tall or short they were, what they weighed ... Basically no one talked about anything that pertained to what any of these people looked like, but everything to do with who they were and how they had treated people.

The stamp that each of these people had left, not only on *my* life but also on the lives of others, was nothing to do with their appearance or their achievements, and everything to do with how they had made me and the other people in their lives *feel*! So why was I still worried about so much of the "small stuff" – the "superficial stuff" – that nobody would remember or care about?

None of the physical attributes that I was obsessed about "fixing" defined who I was or even how the people I loved (and who loved me) saw me. My children wouldn't remember the details of the clothes I wore. My husband's memories of me wouldn't be defined by how textured my skin was. My friends wouldn't recall what dress size I wore. But they *would* all remember the impact that I had on their lives. An impact that would be much greater if I could focus my time and energy on just embracing and loving both them and myself as much as possible, rather than beating myself up about all sorts of trivial things that just don't matter!

This notion of "starting with the end in mind" and realizing just how entirely unimportant so many of the daily things we worry about really are, also allowed me to consider saying all the things that I would about friends and family at their funerals *now*! Why wait until someone is gone to declare how much we love them, or shower them with compliments and encouragement. This tip gave me a whole new valuable perspective on life, so I hope it helps to do the same for you!

Ask, Will it Matter Down the Line?

When I'm complaining or offloading about something, my therapist often asks me "Will it matter five minutes from now?" If I answer yes, she asks, "Five months from now?" This one is a little trickier as, for me, many worries, thoughts and feelings *can* sometimes linger for a fair few months. So if I say yes to this one, she then asks, "What about five years from now?" And I can honestly say that there has been almost nothing going for me at any stage that I could say would categorically matter five years down the line.

Asking yourself these questions – and answering them of course! – is a great reminder of just how little other people's thoughts and opinions are likely to matter as time moves on, and also nudges you to stop "sweating the small stuff".

If you can get into the habit of asking yourself these questions when you're stuck in a rut about something, or when your confidence is wavering or you're feeling unsure about what action to take, your answers can often create the space for you to make a decision with a lot of the fear removed about "if this" or "if that" happened.

If you're anything like me, a lot of the decisions that you are unsure about are as a result of fear. It's crucial that we learn to walk right into the face of fear at times because some of our greatest moments are likely to be waiting to happen just on the other side of it – achievements waiting to be claimed, and a freer, happier life waiting to be lived.

I've learned to use this process for so many things in my life – from making a decision about what dress I want to wear to how I respond to a negative comment from someone. And I love it, as it's a surefire way of helping me to get out of my own way in order to just "go for it" with things, instead of wasting my time away worrying and missing out on all sorts of opportunities.

Emma ran out of time. She didn't have the continued opportunities that many of us do, and I felt like I would have been doing her a disservice if I didn't seize the opportunities that came my way or do the things I wanted, just because I was worried about not seeming "good enough" or about what someone else might say (which is the most common reason by far that we don't do certain things!).

Just to be clear, the idea here isn't to make anyone feel guilty for opportunities that they may not have taken – or indeed to make anyone feel pressured or panicked that they have to take *every* opportunity that comes up. The idea is simply to encourage you to lead a less fearful and more fulfilling life – where you feel less held back by small worries and can fully embrace any opportunities that you *want* to in all their glorious abundance.

I once heard the saying "We miss 100 per cent of the opportunities we don't take". So why not seize as many of them as desired, as who knows which ones might end up changing our lives for the better?

Be Accountable

I used to really struggle with accountability! As I mentioned earlier in the book, I lived so much of my life in my own victimhood, blaming everyone and everything *else* for the feelings that I held about myself, that I was ultimately using it as an excuse to stay stuck in a negative space.

The harsh truth is that so much of us feeling stuck, and not managing to change anything in our lives, is because of nothing or nobody but *ourselves*! Ouch!

Learning to be accountable – not only for the way I was treating myself and the changes that I wanted to make in order to feel better in myself – but also for the impact that I had on other people's lives was a real game changer for me.

This isn't to underestimate the effect that other people can have on us and how we feel at times, of course. But it's about us taking the power back, being in control of where we want to go from here, and confidently claiming responsibility for taking the necessary steps to change our lives for the better.

Take the First Step

When I was looking for hope and motivation for my own journey of change, I came across a lot of incredible people who had transformed their lives. But I often felt that their stories didn't relate to mine and that what they had achieved wasn't obtainable for *me*. I felt like I was just "too average" – and in too deep with my negative thoughts to be able to make real change.

I worried about anything and everything. I allowed myself to be consumed with the idea that those who had made progress were so far ahead of me that it wasn't even worth me even trying. I convinced myself that there was just no point because happiness and confidence were never going to be for *me*. As a result, I stopped myself for a long time from just taking the first step, which is ultimately all that any of us need to do to get the ball rolling ...

We can continue to make excuses and we can continue to allow ourselves to be held back by our self-imposed limitations, or we can take advantage of the gift of time and we can crack the hell on.

You are already the source of hope and power that you're longing for. You just need to give yourself the opportunity to see it.

You will never know the true potential that you have and just how much you are capable of if you continue to live in the confined space created by the limited opinions of others (and/or yourself!). And you will never truly Own your own life if you aren't willing to just take the first step on the path.

YOU GOT THIS

The truth is that it's our fear to truly *Own ourselves* that limits our lives.

Every day that we wake up, we get another opportunity to do whatever we want, to be whoever we want and to Own every little part of who we are.

So let this new way of being start now.

You really only have two choices:

1. You stay where you are. And where I was, was a place of overwhelm, fear and self-doubt, looking everywhere but inside myself for the answers, the healing and the validation that I needed. You probably know that there is something better out there, but can't quite muster up either the courage or the confidence to try to put into action the steps that it will take to find this more fulfilling life – to get to the confident, happy life that you deserve.

OR

2. You make the simple decision to go for it, as you want to Own It! Once you take the first step and knock over the first domino, it leads to all the other incredible pieces of your life starting to fall into place, too – via one small brave decision after another. Remember: life is made up of loads of small decisions, each one leading to another, to another – and each one getting you a step closer to living the life you want to, where you JUST OWN IT. Where you can be you without fear and without worry, and safe in the knowledge that what you bring to the world is needed, wanted and can only be given by you.

I hope you choose Option 2! As only by doing this will you be able to fully OWN IT and become the incredible person that you want to be, are capable of being and absolutely deserve to be!

Thank you for being here and, if no-one has told you already today, you're incredible.

Jess x

Acknowledgements

To my beautiful children – Sophia, Isabella, Jaycen and Baby Boy. Thank you for being my source of joy, unconditional love and sleepless nights! And, ultimately, thank you for making me want to "Own It" so that I can be the best version of me, for you.

To my husband, Trevor – the rock in my life – for embracing me when I am my most authentic self, for encouraging me to never forget who I am, and for supporting all my wild dreams with no hesitation or question.

To my wonderful mother, Elaine – for singlehandedly raising an absolute superstar! For the sacrifices you made, for the confidence you showed me was possible, for leading by example, and for not only being my mother but becoming my best friend. There have been moments in our lives that have been truly dark, but you have risen up, owned them, moved forward and shown me that anything is possible if you just make that first decision to change, take that first step on the path and continue to put one foot in front of the other …

To my little brother, Jordan, and big cousin, Zoe – for always keeping me humble, for loving me unconditionally and for *always* being on the other end of the phone whenever I have needed you.

To Charlotte and Zara, my friends, my support and my go-to girls – thank you for supporting me without judgement (only love), for always reminding me that there is nothing I can't do, and for showing me what sisterhood really is.

To my big and beautiful family – both my Gregorys and my Kings. Thank you all for embracing me and loving me, for giving me a platform to share, celebrate and to feel love. Thank you, too, for being the first to read and share my blogs, for sitting front row at all my events, for clapping harder and cheering louder than anyone else, for never forgetting me and for praying for me.

To Emma – while you may not be Earth-side to read this, thank you for being part of my journey and for letting me be your friend. To your parents, Lesley and Nick, and your brother Darren – for raising Emma to shine her light so bright on all of us, thank you for giving us our Queen Bee.

To my online community – thank you for reminding me constantly why it's ok to be vulnerable, for scooping me up and showering me with love, for supporting my online career and for sharing your personal journeys and stories with me in my DMs. In the moments when I wonder if I have overshared or if anyone is even out there listening, I can almost guarantee that one of you will slide into my DMs and share a change you have made because of something I have said – and I am instantly reminded about why I do what I do. Thank you for every time you choose to follow, like, share and engage with me.

To Beth – thank you for ever thinking that this book was something that I could write and for making it happen!

And to my Viral Talent family – thank you for always having my back and supporting me in all my adventures (and patiently waiting for me to respond to WhatsApp messages!).

ACKNOWLEDGEMENTS

And thank you to *you*, yes *you* – the person reading or listening to this book – for being part of my journey and for being brave enough to start your own journey by having this book in your hands. For having the confidence and courage to even be here. No matter what stage you are at on your journey to Owning It, please know that by buying this book you have been part of making someone else's dreams come true (that'll be mine!) – and that alone makes you bloody awesome.

Useful Resources

Something that I've learned on my journey to Owning It, has been the importance of consistently seeking to learn more, topping up my knowledge from reliable sources. So below are some of the sources that I have loved and learned the most from, and that I cannot recommend highly enough – a combo of inspiring books, useful websites and support networks, and diverse, uplifting social media accounts.

RECOMMENDED READING

- Adegoke, Yomi & Uviebinené, Elizabeth *Slay in your Lane*, Fourth Estate, 2019
- Brown, Brené, *Braving the Wilderness*, Random House, 2017
- Brown, Brené, *Daring Greatly*, Penguin Life, 2015
- Clear, James, *Atomic Habits*, Random House Business, 2018
- Covey, Steven, *The 7 Habits of Highly Effective People*, Free Press, 1989
- Doyle, Glennon, *Untamed*, Vermilion, 2020
- Elman, Michelle, *The Joy of Being Selfish*, Welbeck, 2021
- Gilbert, Elizabeth, *Big Magic*, Bloomsbury, 2016

- Hay, Louise, *Mirror Work*, Hay House, 2016
- Hay, Louise, *You Can Heal Your Life*, Hay House, 1984
- King, Vex, *Good Vibes, Good life*, Hay House, 2018
- Lipton, Bruce *The Biology of Belief*, Hay House, 2015
- Obama, Michelle, *Becoming*, Crown Publishing Group, 2018
- Robbins, Mel, *The 5 Second Rule*, Simon & Schuster, 2017
- Sincero, Jen, *You Are a Badass*, John Murray Learning, 2016
- Victory, Grace, *How to Calm It*, Merky Books, 2021
- Winfrey, Oprah, *What I Know for Sure*, Macmillan, 2014

WEBSITES & SUPPORT NETWORKS

UK

- Dove Self-Esteem Project: www.dove.com/uk/dove-self-esteem-project.html
- Mental Health Foundation UK: www.mentalhealth.org.uk and their body image campaign
- Mind UK: www.mind.org.uk
- Rethink Mental Illness: www.rethink.org
- Samaritans: www.samaritans.org; helpline: 116 123
- Scottish Association for Mental Health (SAMH): www.samh.org.uk
- Shout: www.giveusashout.org; text 85258
- This Girl Can: www.thisgirlcan.co.uk
- Young Minds: www.youngminds.org.uk

Europe

- Mental Health Europe: www.mhe-sme.org
- Mental Health Ireland: www.mentalhealthireland.ie

USA & Canada

- Canadian Mental Health Association: cmha.ca
- Crisis Service Canada: www.ementalhealth.ca
- HelpGuide: www.helpguide.org
- Mentalhealth.gov: www.mentalhealth.gov
- Mental Health America: www.mhanational.org
- National Alliance on Mental Illness (NAMI): www.nami.org
- National Institute of Mental Health: www.nimh.nih.gov
- Very Well Mind: www.verywellmind.com

Australia & New Zealand

- Head to Health: headtohealth.gov.au
- Health Direct: www.healthdirect.gov.au
- Mental Health Australia: mhaustralia.org
- Mental Health Foundation of New Zealand: www.mentalhealth.org.nz
- SANE Australia: www.sane.org

RECOMMENDED SOCIAL MEDIA ACCOUNTS

These Instagram accounts are run by amazing women and organizations – who truly Own It.

I chose not to categorize them under headings such as '"fat activism", "self-love", "confidence", etc, as all these accounts are intersectional and so much more than just one thing. Have a browse, and get your social media plate full of goodness and positivity!

- @_queenmojo
- @aliciamccarvell
- @bespokecurry
- @bodyhappyorg
- @calliethorpe
- @curvy_roamer
- @effyourbeautystandards
- @fashionbellee
- @fatstimbo
- @golden.confidence
- @gracefvictory
- @humanrightswatch
- @humansofny
- @itskellyknox
- @jessontheplussize
- @kat_v_henry
- @luuudaw
- @miss.brielle
- @scarrednotscared
- @selfloveliv
- @sophjbutler
- @stephanieyeboah
- @sydneylbell
- @tessholliday
- @thebirdspapaya
- @thebodiesofwomen
- @theconfidencecorner
- @tobyandroo
- @wheelchair_rapunzel

TriggerHub.org is one of the most elite and scientifically proven forms of mental health intervention

Trigger Publishing is the leading independent mental health and wellbeing publisher in the UK and US. Clinical and scientific research conducted by assistant professor Dr Kristin Kosyluk and her highly acclaimed team in the Department of Mental Health Law & Policy at the University of South Florida (USF), as well as complementary research by her peers across the US, has independently verified the power of lived experience as a core component in achieving mental health prosperity. Specifically, the lived experiences contained within our bibliotherapeutic books are intrinsic elements in reducing stigma, making those with poor mental health feel less alone, providing the privacy they need to heal, ensuring they know the essential steps to kick-start their own journeys to recovery, and providing hope and inspiration when they need it most.

Delivered through TriggerHub, our unique online portal and accompanying smartphone app, we make our library of bibliotherapeutic titles and other vital resources accessible to individuals and organizations anywhere, at any time and with complete privacy, a crucial element of recovery. As such, TriggerHub is the primary recommendation across the UK and US for the delivery of lived experiences.

At Trigger Publishing and TriggerHub, we proudly lead the way in making the unseen become seen. We are dedicated to humanizing mental health, breaking stigma and challenging outdated societal values to create real action and impact. Find out more about our world-leading work with lived experience and bibliotherapy via triggerhub. org, or by joining us on:

 @triggerhub_

@triggerhub.org

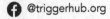 @triggerhub_

Printed in the USA
CPSIA information can be obtained
at www.ICGtesting.com
JSHW031711140824
68134JS00038B/3634

9 781837 962907